Professional
TAROT

About the Author

Christine Jette (pronounced "Jetty") is a registered nurse and holds a bachelor of arts degree in psychology. She is a therapeutic touch practitioner, member of the American Holistic Nurses Association, and professional tarot consultant. Christine teaches writing part-time at the University of Cincinnati and lives with her husband and three cats. Visit Christine at her website: www.findingthemuse.com.

To Write to the Author

If you wish to contact the author or would like more information about this book, please write to the author in care of Llewellyn Worldwide and we will forward your request. Both the author and publisher appreciate hearing from you and learning of your enjoyment of this book and how it has helped you. Llewellyn Worldwide cannot guarantee that every letter written to the author can be answered, but all will be forwarded. Please write to:

Christine Jette
℅ Llewellyn Worldwide
P.O. Box 64383, Dept. 0-7387-0217-X
St. Paul, MN 55164-0383, U.S.A.
Please enclose a self-addressed stamped envelope for reply,
or $1.00 to cover costs. If outside U.S.A., enclose
international postal reply coupon.

Many of Llewellyn's authors have websites with additional information and resources. For more information, please visit our website at: www.llewellyn.com

Professional
TAROT

The Business of Reading, Consulting & Teaching

Christine Jette

2003
Llewellyn Publications
St. Paul, Minnesota 55164-0383, U.S.A.

First Edition
First Printing, 2003

Book design by Joanna Willis
Book editing by Jane Hilken
Cover design by Gavin Dayton Duffy
Cover photo © Mark Adams/Superstock

Library of Congress Cataloging-in-Publication Data
Jette, Christine, 1953–
    Professional tarot: the business of reading, consulting & teaching / Christine Jette.—1st ed.
        p.   cm.
    Includes bibliographical references and index.
    ISBN 0-7387-0217-X
    1. Tarot. I. Title.

    BF1879.T2J475 2003
    133.3'2424—dc21

                                                                    2003044671

Llewellyn Publications
A Division of Llewellyn Worldwide, Ltd.
P.O. Box 64383, Dept. 0-7387-0217-X
St. Paul, MN 55164-0383, U.S.A.
www.llewellyn.com

Printed in the United States of America

Also by Christine Jette

Tarot Shadow Work
Tarot for the Healing Heart
Tarot for All Seasons

For Barbara
and
In memory of Kathleen

Contents

Acknowledgments

I shall become a master in this art only after a great deal of practice.

— Erich Fromm

I signed the contract for *Professional Tarot* in May 2001. I made steady progress on the manuscript until September 11. Like the rest of the world, I watched in horror the unfolding events of that terrible day. About three weeks later, my longtime therapist was killed in a hiking accident. Kathleen fell from a cliff to her death on my birthday. She was my sounding board and objective voice of reason. She guided me through the hills and valleys of writing all my books; I dedicated *Tarot for the Healing Heart* to her. Kathleen's death left a huge hole in my heart.

I lost my ability to concentrate and didn't want to write my own name, let alone a book. As I stared at the computer screen, all I could see was the Tower of tarot: people jumping from the fiery World Trade Center and Kathleen falling to her death. Writing about a pack of cards felt trivial, even absurd. I slid into depression.

The prospective deadline for the manuscript was December 2001. There was no chance I could finish it because I hadn't written a word for over two months. In November I asked Barbara Moore, product development coordinator at Llewellyn, for an extension. As usual, she understood me: "Take the time you need to heal, Christine. Start writing when you feel better." I felt no pressure to "perform" for a buck and turned my full attention to taking care of me. I had some grieving to do.

In early 2002, I resumed writing *Professional Tarot* and a funny thing happened: I started to once again enjoy the writing process. I was looking at the world through a different set of sadder, but wiser, eyes. I revised almost all of what I had written prior to September 11, and the book is (hopefully) better for it. If Barbara had pushed me to crank out a product, I could not have finished the manuscript. Or, if I had completed it, it would have been a joyless obligation. Thank you, Barbara, for giving me exactly what I needed when I needed it—time to heal.

I also want to thank Diane Wilkes for her generous contributions to chapter 3, "Global Tarot," and appendix A, "The Professional Tarot Reader's Code of Ethics." Her web expertise adds depth and understanding to the ever-changing way we communicate with one another and read the cards. Thank you, Diane, for sharing your time and talent with me!

The making of a book is more than writing a manuscript. From cover and interior design to editing, typesetting, and promotion, many people work hard to get my ideas from word processor to bookshelf. Thanks to the attentive staff at Llewellyn for seeing this project through to completion.

Finally, to Tim, my husband, best friend, and the smartest person I have ever known—your humor keeps me humble and our long talks keep me sane. Thank you for loving me enough to always tell me the truth.

Introduction ‖ On the Threshold

Money is congealed energy, and releasing it releases life's possibilities.

— Joseph Campbell

You've been studying the tarot for a long time but wouldn't dream of charging money for a reading. Or, you have been reading for a while but feel inadequate when confronted with a client in crisis. If either of these statements rings true, you are not alone. Many people do occasional tarot readings for money but are stuck on the threshold of developing a professional practice.

There are plenty of tarot books, classes, conferences, and workshops, so a lack of tarot knowledge is not the problem. Over time, I have concluded that two things hold most of us back from becoming professional readers: (1) our ambivalence about charging money for reading the cards, and (2) how to talk to people about the cards—the counseling dimension of a tarot practice.

I have a background in nursing, psychology, energetic healing, teaching, and the tarot. The more I wanted to learn about establishing a professional tarot practice and how to counsel clients during a reading, the more I turned to business, psychology, and astrology books. I began asking, "Why do I have to use an astrology consultation book to learn about professional tarot practices?"

As I lined my bookshelves with astrology, psychology, and business references, it became clear that tarot literature lacked a "how-to-do-readings-for-money" book. Especially lacking were tarot books about setting fees, finding the space to read, marketing, advertising, networking, counseling clients in crisis, reading for teens, teaching a tarot class, legalities of untaxed income, business deductions, using the web to expand a client base, and how to conduct readings that increase client self-awareness.

In this book, I don't draw hard-and-fast rules and I definitely don't pretend to have all the answers. You won't either. The best-trained readers, healers, and psychics in the world don't have all the answers (and if they say they do, get out of there fast!). We all learn by doing, making mistakes, and trying again. My intent is to give you some tools that will guide you on your way as you establish and maintain a thriving, professional tarot practice.

Getting the Most from This Book

If you want to read the cards professionally but are unsure where to begin, or you're a professional reader wanting to improve your business, then *Professional Tarot* is for you. Skim the chapter descriptions below and decide what you want to know now. It doesn't matter if you start in the middle or at the back. Each chapter stands alone.

If you are a true beginner, you may want to read chapter 1 first. It will help you evaluate your skills and assist you in making plans and setting goals. Chapter 6 is also useful to newcomers because it offers tips for learning the tarot and ways to evaluate a tarot teacher. Wherever you begin, may you know abundance and enjoy a prosperous career as a professional tarot consultant.

Chapter 1, "Taking the Leap," assesses the strengths and challenges of a professional tarot reader and examines attitudes and beliefs about money. Abundance is an outlook: you learn how to draw the energy of money to you for success.

We need money to be socially acceptable, but it is not socially acceptable to be too eager to make it. Money is an emotionally charged issue and is assigned tremendous power, especially when someone is coming to you for help and you have to discuss money first. As a professional reader, you need to understand the culture of money and the value you place on your services. Finally, you will explore the myth of competition and learn how to carve out a niche market that expresses the one-and-only you.

Chapter 2, "Building Your Tarot Practice," begins by helping you decide what to charge for your services and how to talk to clients about money. You'll learn safety precautions when reading in the home and find creative places to read. By keeping a "tarot-to-go" kit ready, you'll never miss a spontaneous opportunity to make money when you encounter people who want readings on the spur of the moment.

Chapter 2 also examines the difference between promotion and hype. "Getting the word out" about tarot services involves advertising. You'll explore the law of supply and demand and develop the skill of knowing what your clients need. Practical considerations include naming your business, low-cost ways to advertise, referring clients to another reader, and having a contingency plan for unexpected events.

In chapter 3, "Global Tarot," you explore phone consultations, including how to recognize at-risk callers and building a tarot practice in cyberspace. The Internet is constantly evolving. Today's technology is tomorrow's obsolete software. For this reason, chapter 3 doesn't cover the specifics of how to build your own website. Instead, it offers general guidelines to get you started. Please refer to appendix C for resources providing specific information.

"The Business of Tarot" covers the legalities of being in business for yourself. Chapter 4 examines zoning and licensing laws, keeping legal records, untaxed income, using a computer for business purposes, and the practical and legal considerations of closing your practice. You'll also learn how to work smarter with barter and organize your office space.

Chapter 5, "Counseling Clients," explores the psychological aspects of reading for another. On the surface, people have tarot readings for fun, on a whim, out of curiosity, to be entertained, to catch a glimpse of the future, or just to talk about life. On a deeper level, people have tarot readings because they want a private place to talk about problems, reveal secrets, or discuss concerns. Knowledge of psychology and counseling techniques is needed to handle emotionally charged issues with intelligence. This knowledge allows you to phrase a reading so that the client can relate to the information and feel empowered to change what is no longer useful, or build upon existing strengths.

A professional reader's ability to help a client is limited by many factors, and a client's problems are often not within the scope of a tarot reading. A professional reader is able to distinguish between a "normal" crisis (stressful but predictable parts of life) and a true emergency such as the threat of suicide. The focus of "Counseling Clients" is on recognizing a true crisis, maintaining a state of calm, knowing what to do, and keeping a list of healthcare resources close by, including emergency numbers.

If you do short readings in quick succession all day long, you'll find a helpful section in chapter 5 titled "The Ten-Minute Reader." Even if you are giving five-minute, one-card readings, you still need to find a focus and begin and end well. Ending a short reading with grace and style can be tricky. Chapter 5 concludes with a look at special considerations when reading for minors.

Teaching others how to read the tarot is creative, enjoyable, and downright frightening, if you're not well prepared. It requires a commitment of time and energy. Adult learners want information that is accurate, concise, and immediately applicable. Chapter 6, "Teaching—and Learning—Tarot," explores the keys to successful teaching with suggestions for organizing the class in a workshop format geared to the needs of adults. To gain objectivity, you'll learn to evaluate your tarot class through the eyes of a student.

In "The Energy to Succeed," the epilogue looks at psychic and emotional burnout and provides help for the helper. The three appendices offer a professional tarot reader's code of ethics, compliments of web mistress Diane Wilkes; sample outlines of a six-week beginner tarot course and an advanced specialty class; and conclude with a list of my favorite tarot resources, both online and off. Think of *Professional Tarot* as a planning guide to open again and again as you stand on the threshold, build a thriving practice, and prosper. Enjoy the journey.

1 || Taking the Leap

Trust that still small voice that says, "This might work and I'll try it."

— Diane Mariechild

In this chapter, you'll assess the strengths and challenges of a professional tarot reader and examine attitudes and beliefs about money. Abundance is an outlook: you learn how to draw the energy of money to you for success. As a professional reader, you will examine the culture of money and the value you place on your services. You will also explore the myth of competition and learn how to carve out a niche market that expresses the one-and-only you. Let's begin with a scary proposition.

A Scary Proposition

People tend to get tarot readings at a time of indecision or personal crisis. They are vulnerable to suggestions and are looking for advice. Knowledge is power. As professional readers, we have the power to influence our clients because people in need tend to hang on to every word we say. This is a scary proposition for a lot of us because it carries awesome responsibility. Two things can happen: we either charge headfirst into a situation we are not prepared for and it blows up in our face, or we doubt our own abilities and never take the leap of faith needed to become a professional reader.

Here are some of the most common beliefs that hold us back from success as professional readers.

I'm not . . .
>good enough, talented enough, smart enough, etc.
>psychic.
>[*fill in the blank*].

I can't . . .
>charge money for reading the cards.
>make a living as a tarot reader.
>[*fill in the blank*].

I don't know . . .
>where to start.
>how to find clients.
>[*fill in the blank*].

I must . . .
>have all the answers.
>fix everything.
>be able to tell the client what to do.
>take responsibility for my client's problems.
>[*fill in the blank*].

Professional Tarot explores these self-limiting beliefs in depth. Read on.

Why Do You Want to Be a Professional Tarot Reader?

It is important to be clear about your motives and intentions before you read the tarot cards for another person. Why do you want to be a pro? Stop and really think about this. Make an entry in your journal. To get you started, the following are some possible reasons for becoming a professional tarot reader. Bear in mind that this is not an all-inclusive list.

I want to become a professional tarot card reader in order to

- help the client gain greater insight and objectivity about a situation;

- help the client discover new solutions to old problems;

- empower the client to face changes with courage;

- educate the client about the value of tarot as a tool for spiritual growth and awareness;

- make money;

- gain personal satisfaction in helping others;

- increase intuitive skills and knowledge;

- enhance personal growth and increase self-esteem;

- make a reputation for myself, have increased popularity, and gain well-deserved attention;

- become an authority in the field;

- be more fully alive and engaged in a magical life;

- [*insert your own reasons here*].

Oil and Water

I have volunteered for various causes throughout my life. Everyone is happy to have my free services, time, and skills. Several years ago, after two years of volunteer work, I very much wanted to become a paid employee for a certain organization. As soon as I mentioned money, everything changed. My qualifications were immediately in question. I found this puzzling because I was asking to be paid for the job I had done for two years as a volunteer. I learned there is a big difference between doing something for free and charging for those same services.

No tarot book can equal the experience of doing actual readings. Reading free for friends is a great way to practice and fine-tune your skills. Friends are patient with the learning process and tolerant of shortcomings. Reading for relatives and friends who want you to succeed creates a positive atmosphere. You have an added edge during a reading because you already know something about them. Without charging money, a reading has no strings attached and can be all in fun.

But at some point, you may feel you are skilled enough to charge something. For paid readings, you may be starting with people you know, friends, or coworkers. The old saying goes that friends and money don't mix, especially if you have been doing free readings for them. Asking for money from a friend can be awkward.

Charging a fee encourages you to fine-tune your skills to increase competency. Slapdash methods of mediocrity are okay when your readings are free. You work harder at a reading when people are paying you for it. As a L'Oréal commercial might phrase it, you charge money for your readings because "you're worth it."

Only you can decide if you will charge money when reading for friends. Money has destroyed more than one relationship, and just like oil and water, friends and money mix with difficulty. My advice is once you do start charging for tarot readings, it's not a good idea to revert back to free sessions; it may feel like charity to your friends and it comes across as condescension on your part.

You will also have friends who expect freebies because you are "buddies." If you find yourself in this situation, please fast-forward to the section called "Are You Funny About Money?" later in this chapter. It explores beliefs and attitudes that get in the way of prosperity.

You will find most people do not like to be rescued because it does not honor their ability to help themselves. If you're starting out and doing a reading for a friend, suggest that your friend do something for you in return, even if it's just buying you a cappuccino. I have found that people get less out of a free reading because they value the advice less. The old adage stands true—you get what you pay for.

Increasing Confidence

The methods of increasing your confidence while reading the tarot can be summarized in one word: practice! Back in the dinosaur era when I started reading the tarot cards, potential seekers were almost extinct, or at least on the endangered species list. I was forced to invent creative ways to practice and increase my confidence. I had imaginary clients: I'd do a layout and give a reading while pretending someone was actually sitting at the table with me. (You may want to close your drapes while you sit at a table talking to yourself . . .)

I looked at pictures of friends or family members while I read for them in their absence. I heard of people in the news and did readings for them at my imaginary consultation table. I called friends and asked if I could do a reading, then I taped it and mailed it to them. Record your readings, real or imagined. You can learn a lot by listening to how you sound to others. It's another way to develop the narrative so necessary in reading the tarot.

Every day I carried a different tarot card in my pocket and tried to see if it fit any situation in my life, or I observed if anyone I encountered during the day was the essence of the card. I looked at the card on my breaks and lunch hour or standing in line. The opportunities to practice are limited only by your imagination.

Over the years, I have discovered that people are open to direction and help in life because none of us can completely figure it out. Read for anyone and everyone who will let you because this develops your style, allows you to improve your presentation, and confirms your readiness to charge money. You will be surprised at how receptive most people are to the novelty of it. Take your books with you. Tell them you are learning. If you get stuck, open your books. As long as you are honest about the process of learning and don't charge money with your books open, people won't mind. After all, you are discussing a topic of interest—them.

There's That Word Again

At the risk of sounding like a CD stuck on track one, *practice* makes a perfectly competent tarot reader. The following suggestions will get you started on your path to becoming a professional reader:

- Have your own reading done by an established professional. Note the narrative and how the cards relate to one another. Decide what you liked and disliked about the style and presentation.

- Work with only one or two layouts at first until the positions are firmly in your mind. You might want to choose one general and one specific layout that "ring true" to you. Any layout from any source can be used if you feel "right" about it.

- Keep it simple. Count the number of major arcana cards in a spread and note the minor arcana suits. This will tell you a lot about the general "theme" of a reading without interpreting individual cards. Stating the "theme" is a great way to open a narrative.

- Keep reference books within reach. Begin memorizing "catch phrases" for each of the cards. For instance, my catch phrase for the Hermit is "going within." Having a one- or two-word phrase to fall back on is handy when you find yourself having brain cramps or drawing a complete blank. Sometimes, just saying the memorized catch phrase is all you need to get the information flowing.

- If you are stuck on a card's meaning, begin by describing the card. For example, the World is in the "future" position of your spread and you can't for the life of you remember what it means. Look at the card and describe it something like this: "Your body language is open and you look happy, almost as though you were floating or dancing. You are embracing the world. It's in the 'future' position, so the trend shows an open and happy time for you." This description is very close to the meaning of the World and will start the narrative flowing so you can discern the card's significance for the seeker.

- Speak out loud and record every reading. As you listen to yourself on tape, try to visualize the layout and see the cards in their positions.

- If you are doing a make-believe reading or taping a reading for an absent friend, imagine what the client would ask about the cards. (See chapter 5.)

- Answer all questions with as much honesty as you can. By being truthful and saying what the seeker needs to know (as opposed to what the seeker wants to know), you will never have a false frame of reference and never get caught in that tangled web we weave when first we practice to deceive.

- Summarize a reading in three minutes or less. Practice closure and firmly saying time is up. Ending a reading is often more difficult than starting one.

- Avoid the temptation to appear all-knowing, because none of us knows it all. Anyway, do you really want to take responsibility for someone else's life?

- Begin contemplating the type of atmosphere you want for your readings. Soothing? Healing? Mysterious? Spiritual? Business-like? Therapeutic? Sacred? Entertaining? Will you use incense, candles, or have crystals on your reading table?

- One of the best ways to develop skill as a reader is to open your life to intuition. Memorizing traditional definitions of the cards keeps you out of fantasy and wishful thinking; traditional meanings are a great safety net when you draw a complete blank. But the magic of tarot lies in combining traditional meanings with intuitive skill so you can customize a reading to the individual. This is accomplished only when you trust your voice of inner knowing.

- Many wonderful books are written about developing psychic ability. My favorites are in appendix C. For me, however, it's a short book: Ask for guidance from the Highest Source in the most understandable form possible for the good of all, expect to receive it, then stand out of the way and accept the *first thought* that comes into your head. That's it. Learning to absolutely trust the first thought that pops into your head is the hardest part. Blending logic, common sense, sound communication skills, and intuition is tricky. It takes—you guessed it—practice.

Become a Lifelong Learner

If you want to be a good tarot reader, you need to know more than the meaning of the cards; you need to know about life. The more you know, the better your ability to interpret the cards in a way that is relevant to the client. Just studying the tarot isn't enough. You may have an encyclopedic knowledge of the tarot, but if you don't understand people and how to reach them, you won't be an effective professional reader.

For example, in a reading you might say the Four of Cups means depression or feeling like an opportunity has been missed and you rush right past this to the next position. If you know about counseling techniques, you could stop and ask, "Have you been feeling depressed lately?" Drawing the client into a narrative of his or her own reading yields far more useful information about the cards' meanings than breezily placing yourself in the position of the all-knowing, mysterious High Priestess.

When I read for others, I draw my clients into talking about themselves by asking questions. It's their reading, not mine. I know this method is not for everyone, but consider the following example: When you go to a doctor, do you say, "Hey, Doc, I've been having symptoms. Why don't you divine what they are for me?" Nope, you give the good doctor as much personal information as you can, enabling the physician to give intelligent advice in return. It also holds true for a tarot reading. The more information you garner from your client, the more meaningful and helpful the reading will be.

The insight and skills needed to translate the tarot cards are similar to counseling techniques. Knowledge of psychology and counseling is indispensable when reading the cards for others. As obvious as this sounds, in order for a reading to be useful to your client, it has to make sense to that person. People want practical advice about their problems. If you go "cosmic" with your interpretations, you run the risk of confusing rather than helping, and just how useful is that?

I'm not suggesting you go back to college and get another degree, but you will be better prepared to offer responsible advice if you go to a library or bookstore on a regular basis. Read books about counseling and psychology, take a course, and attend workshops. Listen to successful radio advice shows. The advisor has the responsibility to keep the caller on track and offer closure in a respectful, but timely, fashion. Listen to how the "experts" handle questions that are outside their areas of expertise. Any educational experience that teaches how to give sound advice can teach you a lot about giving such advice during a professional tarot session.

The Myths of Owning Your Own Business

The benefits of owning your own business are obvious: you're in charge, you can set your own schedule and choose your own coworkers, and it's exciting to take a risk. Understand that you are contemplating a major life change that requires courage.

The drawbacks of being in business for yourself may be less obvious: no paid benefits, no sick time, no guaranteed income, playing all the roles from president to janitor and every job in between. Before we go one step further, let's clear up some misunderstandings about the glories of owning your own business.[1]

- Myth 1: *You're the boss*. You are also the janitor, receptionist, financial advisor, accountant, bookkeeper, secretary, publicist, and marketing expert. As sole proprietor with a staff of one, the appropriate question becomes, "The boss of what?"

- Myth 2: *You'll make lots of money right away*. It takes time to build your loyal clientele; becoming a prosperous tarot reader doesn't happen overnight. Don't quit your day job while you prepare, advertise, and network.

- Myth 3: *You can avoid office politics.* Well, there are certainly no politics in my own office for one, but anytime you do business consultations or read at a retail store or psychic fair, you risk bumping into internal turmoil, sometimes in a most uncomfortable way. You never know when you're going to tap into someone else's personal issues.

- Myth 4: *You'll work fewer hours.* This is the biggest myth of all. Making a tarot consultation service grow takes a huge commitment of time and energy. When your earnings are in direct proportion to your output, you feel compelled to stay at it.

- Myth 5: *You won't have to take orders.* Certainly no one will be standing over you telling you how to read the cards. But, for the amount of time you are dealing with a client, each one of them is your boss because they are hiring you, specifying the type of reading they want, paying you, and evaluating your performance. Your clients can make or break your success as a professional reader by word-of-mouth comments.

- Myth 6: *You can watch the kids while you work.* If you want to run a serious business, you have to arrange the same kind of childcare or babysitting you would if you worked for an employer. No one can pay attention to a baby and a client at the same time.

- Myth 7 (for night owls only): *You can sleep late.* When I quit my job as a registered nurse with its ghastly starting time of 7 A.M., I had visions of throwing my alarm clock away. Harsh reality descended upon me quickly: the world still operated on a nine-to-five schedule. People who phone at 9 A.M. and get only your voice mail are frequently hard to reach the rest of the day. Even though I am perky at 10 P.M., it is still a tough time to return business calls. I am free to work at any hour, but if I want to interact with the rest of the world, I have to be functional in the morning.

The Power of Three

The three core personality traits for establishing a successful business are belief in self, the willingness to work, and a desire to be of service to others.[2] Try a meditative journal exercise I call "The Power of Three." Pull the Queen of Wands, Pentacles, and Cups from your favorite deck. Have them in sight as you do this activity.

Underneath the Queen of Wands write "Belief in Self." Below the Queen of Pentacles write "Willingness to Work." "Desire to Be of Service to Others" belongs to the Queen of Cups. Read the following comments about each one, then look at her card as you pen your personal response to each Queen.

1. Belief in Self (Queen of Wands)

What do you believe? One way to identify your beliefs is to ask yourself what might happen if you actually did manifest a successful tarot consultation service. Do you worry you may be asking for too much or feel unworthy to realize your dream? Does bringing change into your life make you nervous? How will success change your life?

The Queen of Wands is businesslike and exuberant about everything she does. She has reserves of energy and is passionate about things she believes in. She devours details and follows her hunches because she trusts her intuition. The Queen of Wands believes in herself. So the real question here is, "How good can you stand it?" That's as good as it gets. Make an entry in your journal.

2. Willingness to Work (Queen of Pentacles)

How much elbow grease are you willing to apply to make your dream real? Willingness to work requires that you identify and eliminate everything that keeps you from focusing on your dream. It means finding the time and discipline to establish the order that a successful business must have to grow. Chaos, clutter, and unfinished business on any level are energy bandits. Every moment you spend looking for things, apologizing for being late, or mentally hiding out from unfinished business is time you have lost forever.

The Queen of Pentacles is infinitely practical, a go-getter, and is comfortable in both the home and the office. She also listens to what her body is telling her. If she is hungry, she eats, and she rests when tired. She takes care of herself in every way. By replenishing her reserves, she makes room for new energy and the creative life force to flow.

Desire equals discipline and there is no such thing as a free lunch, but the Queen of Pentacles succeeds by balancing work and personal life. Her life does not appear more unstable than the lives of her clients. Instincts and logic work together and she empowers others by empowering herself first. Make an entry in your journal.

3. Desire to Be of Service to Others (Queen of Cups)

How much are you willing to love? When you choose to bring love and enthusiasm into your tarot practice, the whole process takes on a magical and healing quality. You stop hitting a brick wall. When you introduce love and enthusiasm into your work, it will remove obstacles and help you find balance.

Bringing love into your choices as you work toward your goal of being a professional reader draws in the support of the universe. When you are enthusiastic and loving, divine support will join you. This is about power. Not the kind of power that erupts out of the personal ego, but the kind that gracefully flows through you when you tap into the powerful, loving support of the universe.

The Queen of Cups is filled with compassion and her nurturing extends to all who come into her realm. She excels in metaphysics, accepts her natural psychic abilities, and makes a marvelous professional tarot reader. The Queen of Cups's nature is spiritual and loving, and her work must be emotionally satisfying. She practices the spiritual law of "give and it shall be given to you." This Queen understands the law of cause and effect. She is generous in her kindness to others because she knows that as she gives, it will return to her a thousandfold.

When you expand your heart and generous spirit, you expand your capacity to be happy and fulfilled and to operate from a sense of

abundance. Thoughts are real. Let your thoughts be of divine awareness, rightfully expecting and easily sharing all the gifts the universe
has to offer you. Surround yourself with supportive and loving family
and friends. As a professional tarot reader, you can help many people
deepen their connection to the divine and gain clarity about their
chosen paths. Be proud of what you do as you prepare for positive life
changes. Make an entry in your journal.

Discovering Your Personal Style and Voice

We are all different. We come from different life experiences and have
talents or outlooks that are ours alone. What type of tarot reading do
you enjoy when you are having one for yourself? What type of reading
turns you off? If you can clearly describe them, you will have a key to
understanding your strengths as well as your challenges, and the type
of reader you want to be based on your natural abilities.

I get a reading from an objective practitioner about twice a year. I
call it "checking in with the universe." Over the years, I have had readings from world-famous psychics and local professionals. I began taking notes on the variety of styles and presentations. Even though an
infinite number of nuances exist in presentation, I believe there are
four basic styles of reading the cards for another: teaching, interpreting, healing, and mystic. I also propose that a fifth type of reader exists
on the ideal plane. I will call her the alchemist.

Read over the descriptions that follow and see what type of reader
(or combination of types) you are. To help you decide, I have chosen
the Ace of Pentacles as an example and each section describes how the
teacher, interpreter, healer, or mystic responds to the card. Which meaning sounds right to you? It will be the one that "rings true" with your
inner wisdom as you read it, so trust your intuition as you scan the
descriptions. None is better or worse than another. They simply detail
different ways of reading the cards.

Please note: The English language does not provide me with a pro-
noun that means he *or* she. I do not mean to exclude half the human

race in my descriptions. But I also don't want to drive you crazy switching back and forth between he and she. I have solved the dilemma by staying with "her" throughout. My apologies to the gentlemen who are reading this book!

The Teacher

The teacher loves giving information, dispensing knowledge, and increasing a client's ability to help herself. She is articulate and communicative. The teacher asks questions, is interactive and jovial, but with friendly detachment. She solves problems through logic and imagination. Hint: You are a teacher if you relish the idea of teaching a tarot class and looked at chapter 6 first.

If you are a teacher, you respond to client questions by asking your own questions, rather than offering direct advice in a reading. You see your role as teaching people how to learn about themselves and solve their own problems through self-understanding. You would rather teach a person how to fish than invite her to a fish dinner. If the Ace of Pentacles turns up in a reading, the teacher asks, "Do you believe conditions are favorable for taking the next step in any projects you are considering? How does work contribute to your feelings of security?"

Your strengths include working with small, informal groups. You love one-on-one interactions. Marketing is easy for you because you excel in communication skills. You have the ability to empower people through their own efforts and know how to laugh at life's absurdities. Challenges for the teacher include the tendency to become a nag or know-it-all, and to possess a detachment that lacks empathy for your client's emotional pain.

The Interpreter

Interpreters have no intent to control and they accept the cards at face value. They play with the information that is already there, building upon it in new ways by elaborating. An interpreter improves the original plan because she tends to work on what's there, rather than creating something new. Interpreters don't make the product, they make the existing product better. Hint: You are an interpreter if you read an idea in this book and see the end result in a step-by-step, orderly process.

In a reading, the interpreter can envision an outcome but is patient enough to work on an outcome detail by detail. If the Ace of Pentacles appears, you not only see the positive financial outcome of a client's situation, but can also suggest detailed steps to get there. You will be able to rattle off a pertinent "list of things to do" to carry your client to her goal.

The interpreter's greatest gift is her ability in the role of consultant, because she combines intellect with visionary genius. Interpreters excel at elaborating on possible outcomes and are able to see how a situation will evolve. They don't want to change the existing idea or plan, but want to make the existing plan better. If a current situation needs to be scrapped, it can become a problem for the interpreter because there is a tendency to resist letting go and starting over.

The Healer

Healers have an impulse toward service and giving. They want to console, nurture, and fix things. They are intuitive rather than logical and have a strong sense of their own code for living. Many healers have had tumultuous experiences that lend special insight into life's complexities. Hint: You are a healer if one of your favorite expressions is "I know how you feel." You take your emotional pain and make sense of it for the benefit of others.

Readings slant toward the physical body or psychological/emotional/spiritual healing. Healers can't look at a tarot card without seeing its healing potential. When the healer sees the Ace of Pentacles in a reading, her immediate response might be, "You're on the road to recovery. You can speed things along by consulting an herbalist. It also suggests you are on the first step to a more satisfying attitude about work."

The healer's greatest strength springs from sensitivity to emotional pain. They are empathetic listeners and reserve judgment because they have "been there." After a reading, the client may well believe she has finally found someone who understands and is willing to listen.

Of course, healers can have big challenges in a professional setting. Because of an increased emotional sensitivity, there is a risk of job burnout or depression. In teaching, a healer may want to do everything for the class, which doesn't allow for personal exploration. She can be smothering or controlling because she wants to "fix" everything and make it all better. Marketing can be difficult for the healer because of sensitivity to criticism.

The Mystic

Like healers, mystics engage their personal code of ethics and spiritual beliefs. Mystics understand the relationship between spirituality and creativity. They live a life of simplicity and are independent thinkers driven by a burning spiritual search. Hint: You are a mystic if you stare out the window absorbed in the details of your senses. You are comfortable alone in silence and your hunger for a better world colors your everyday actions. Your favorite saying is "As above, so below." If the spiritual search is your highest value, you can bet you are a mystic.

During readings, mystics create moods and ambience. They may have an exquisite amethyst crystal on the table with fresh flowers, heady incense, glowing candles, and soft music. And you can be assured that each item has a spiritual purpose. They deal with small, detailed observations and feelings. Mystics are ephemeral, constantly processing all experiences (both mundane and magical) through the lens of a spiritual eye.

If the Ace of Pentacles shows up in a reading, a mystic will ask about the relationship of the card between the personal and the universal. What is its larger focus? The mystic might ask, "How will your new work endeavor benefit you spiritually? Will your new project be spiritually fulfilling?"

The mystic's strengths include the ability to give equal attention to intuition and logic. They can see the grand scheme and the small details at once because mystics give each equal time. There is no difference between the two. They possess purity of vision and strength of conviction. Mystics can connect to clients in intimate, creative ways and excel in past-life readings.

Mystics, as well-intentioned as they are, can get caught in the trap of blaming, New Age style. Because everything has a cosmic reason to the mystic, there is a tendency to discount the pain of immediate suffering. For example, a mystic reader may tell a rape victim that she was raped because she is paying back a karmic debt. This does nothing to help the victim's immediate pain and actually makes the situation worse: "Oh, the rape was my fault." Not only does this disempower the rape victim, but it also offers no practical solutions to the current suffering except assigning blame.

Mystics also can fall into the trap of being "feel-good" readers. Because everything is impossibly decided by fate, don't worry about it. It will all work out in the end. It's for the best, according to cosmic reason. Telling a client that her breast cancer will be okay because it fits into a karmic plan is not altogether useful. It does nothing to help the client *now* and, once again, does not empower a client to take action on her own behalf. Nothing in tarot is preordained and mystics must work hard to remember this.

Because mystics do not value conventional categories, they are often unwilling to work the system. Marketing is difficult for them. Mystics detest networking and schmoozing because it feels dishonest. They may indeed have a tendency to cut off their nose to spite their face due to fierce independent thinking. Mystic readers should start small with any marketing endeavor and only advertise what they believe to be true. They could meditate for creative ideas about their business and write them down. They would do well to be true to themselves above all.

Mystics do best with a gentle work environment. They thrive on lots of privacy and a pleasant ambience. They need to develop rituals that feel right to them. Mystics do not enjoy the limelight and do not need positive strokes as much as some. Their sense of self-worth is an inside job. If you are a mystic reader, try teaching one-on-one or through mail correspondence. Keep personal contacts at a minimum and cherish your alone time. Consider online tarot consultations to match to your personality and specialize in past-life readings.

The Alchemist

Earlier I proposed that there is a fifth type of reader. The alchemist is a careful blending of all types and represents an ideal. She takes the friendly detachment and ability to empower from the teacher, the logic of the interpreter, the intuitive nurturing of the healer, and the mystic's ability to see the big picture through the details. The alchemist is able to respond to the needs of a client by working on all levels. I may never be an alchemist in my professional practice, but the goal is what keeps me searching, striving, learning, and growing with the tarot. What type of reader are you? What are your strengths and challenges? Make an entry in your journal.

The Myth of Competition and Finding Your Niche as a Reader

True or false: (1) The only places you can read the cards for money are at psychic festivals, New Age bookstores, street fairs, bars, or coffeehouses. (2) You must compete with a lot of other readers for a client's attention. (3) With so many readers in one place, you'll be lucky to break even and recoup the table fee. All false!

Professional tarot readers who fear competition are way off base, because we each can create our own niche and therefore our own market. There is no scarcity of new clients, only a scarcity of tarot readers with the imagination and know-how to go out and find them. The biggest mistake professional tarot readers make is not tapping into new markets. What about your life circumstances makes you special? In what way do you stand out from the crowd of other tarot readers? If you incorporate your individual creativity with your other passions, you will triple your chances of success as a professional.

Tarot reading is essentially the same everywhere, but tarot readers are different. Think through your life experiences to find out who you are, what you've done, and what you have to offer. Discovering your uniqueness based on your history, background, set of skills, and natural talent is a springboard to sharing the divinely inspired you with the rest of the world.

To get you started thinking about individual creativity, I'll share how I have put my background to work for me. I am a registered nurse with a degree in psychology and a hands-on healer. I have found a niche of using the tarot cards for healing. I combine a chakra-based reading with a hands-on energetic treatment that clients find soothing. Because my education slants to the counseling aspect of the cards, I aim for accurate, empathetic readings. Shared experience—being heard and understood—creates a bond that is healing in a way no literal translation of the cards can replace. I also taught nursing assistants for many years, so teaching a tarot class is a natural for me. Enough about me. Let's examine the one-and-only you.

All your life history has potential. Suppose you are devoting your life to raising your child. Your skills give you much to offer other parents. Did you take care of an elderly parent? You have the experience to assist people confronting the stresses of an aging parent. If you've survived the death of a loved one, you can listen to a client's pain with empathy and specialize in bereavement counseling.

Battered wives and incest survivors can use their history to help others working through the same experiences. If you're in recovery, you have something to teach others with similar problems. You can say, "Look, I've been there," without coming across as preaching on high moral ground.

A word to the wise: In *Tarot for the Healing Heart,* I write about the wounded healer.[3] We cannot heal another until we ourselves are healed. You can help another in pain only if you've done some healing for yourself. I mean actually working it out in therapy, self-help groups, reading, bodywork, meditation, past-life regression, herbal remedies, whatever works for you.

In chapter 5, "Counseling Clients," we will examine ineffective readings, a quality I call "inflicting a reading on another." You wouldn't reveal the gory details of your past to your client—it's not *your* session and too much revelation suggests a lack of professional boundaries. For now, understand that passing on any unresolved feelings during a session seriously affects your ability to help your client.

Pain and horrific experiences aren't the only niche-makers in the tarot market! What are you interested in? What is your *special slant* to the tarot cards? What will make you stand out from the crowd? Start thinking *combinations*. Possible combinations include: tarot *and* . . . aromatherapy; massage; astrology; feng shui; herbs; spell work; polarity balancing; financial planning; companion animal communication; past-life regressions; hypnosis; vocational, nutritional, teen, or spiritual counseling; relationship advisor; healing; art therapy; business planning. Well, you get the idea. The possibilities for finding a niche market are endless.

What kind of jobs have you had? If you've worked in retail, banking, business, daycare, gardening, at a pet shelter or as a pet-sitter—anything at all—you can turn your work experience into a potential niche market for professional tarot reading.

Slay the myth of the competition dragon once and for all. Yes, it's easier to stay stuck in the same old place, reading the same old way, sweating it out in a room full of other readers, hoping you'll clear expenses. Please don't misunderstand: this type of reading is valuable and requires incredible skill and endurance. But, in the long run, it emphasizes competition with other readers *because you are doing the same thing they are doing.*

It is more work to be creative and offer something fresh and new, but there is enough prosperity out there for all of us. You need never compete with other readers again. Take a moment to answer the following questions, and you'll be well on your way to carving out a niche market in tarot that expresses the one-and-only you:

- Who are you?

- What have you done?

- What do you have to offer?

- What jobs have you had?

- What do you want to learn?

- How much are you willing to work to carve out a niche market?

- What are you good at?

- What do you enjoy?

Okay, you've read this section and discover that you have a *potential* niche market but you're not there yet. If so, do not pass go, do not collect two hundred dollars. Immediately reread the previous section called "Become a Lifelong Learner." In order to be good at the identified niche market, you may have to read a few books, research, take a course or workshop, develop the material—or heal some more. Take what you know and work with it. Grab every example and thoroughly examine it. Articulate what you know. In no time, you'll be ready for chapter 2, as you slant your ad or brochure so others will be drawn to your unique knowledge.

Are You Funny About Money?

Ah, the proverbial rock and hard place! It is perfectly acceptable to want money and not so acceptable to be overly eager to make it. Please understand that there is a difference between greed, prosperity, and profit. Greed is taking without giving back and suggests a selfish imbalance. Greed isn't about how much we have, but how little we give.

We need enough money to continue putting forth our efforts as tarot readers; that is, to continue offering our services. Profit is a financial term for having enough money to continue giving back. Prosperity is a balanced feeling of well-being grounded in the cycle of giving and taking.

Money is an emotionally charged energy. Think for a moment about how easy it is to get angry when you disagree with your bank's statement or feel you were overcharged at the checkout line. Money is personal. More friendships, relationships, and partnerships are destroyed by money disputes than for any other reason. When people ask, "What do you charge?" they are really asking, "What are you worth?"

There is ambivalence among New Age practitioners about charging for service work that has a divine dimension. We are tempted to charge less than we are worth because we fear we won't have clients or they won't come back if our prices are too high. In other words, we don't charge enough because we don't deserve it. Try this journal entry to clear up old beliefs and inner blocks that stand in the way of you and success:

1. Why do I want money?

2. How do I feel about money?

3. What will it take for me to have all the money I want?

4. What will I need to give in order to have money?

5. What will I need to receive in order to have money?

6. How will having more money change my life and the lives of my loved ones?

7. What will I be able to do with more money that I cannot do now?

8. What do I think and feel about others who have lots of money?

9. What will happen if I get what I work for?

10. What new responsibilities will I have by making lots of money?

As women, we may have grown up with the idea that we are "supposed" to take care of people and it comes up again as adults when someone needs us. We fall into the parenting role because we have had lots of practice meeting the needs of others without asking for anything in return. Our clients will call on us at any time of the day or

night; we may not charge them because of our need (or social pro-
gramming) to nurture.

Women in any profession are still underpaid in comparison to men.
We have to work a little harder to show our competence, but it is
"unattractive" to be a leader. A more subtle reason that women are paid
less than men is because we *ask* for less! In *Kiss My Tiara*, author Susan
Jane Gilman writes that men negotiate salaries better and demand
more money. They also lobby for raises and women don't. We're just
grateful someone hired us.[4] Low self-esteem, with its corresponding
low expectations, is a theme among women. We undervalue our work
and worth.

We talk about self-esteem, but demonstrate the opposite. The only
way to walk the walk is to charge what we are worth. If we want to talk
about self-esteem, we must first learn to practice it. Wake up, ladies:
Prosperity is not male. Please learn to value your worth as a tarot
reader and charge accordingly.

I can't leave the "funny about money" section without mentioning
dysfunctional backgrounds. One of my favorite cartoons depicts a
large auditorium with an overhead banner that reads "National Adult
Children of Normal Parents Convention." There is one person in the
great hall. I am convinced that we are *all* "recovering from life" to
some degree.

People with dysfunctional backgrounds, such as alcoholic or abusive
parenting, usually have a problem with self-worth. This low self-esteem
may make it especially difficult to feel entitled to charge enough money
for services. Adult children from addictive families may end up with
either ungrounded, grandiose ideas about money that stem from not
feeling safe or never being satisfied or able to get enough; or, they may
be overly cautious and driven, in an attempt to establish safety.[5]

Once you have the confidence to deliver a smooth presentation,
there *should* be a fee. (Please reread this last sentence until you believe
it.) You are not selling content or information, for this would hold you
hostage to always telling the client what she *wants* to hear; but you are
selling your ability and time. Your abilities are acquired through study,

effort, and discipline. You are offering a skilled service. A person whose business involves rendering a service is selling time as well as skill and expertise. This service deserves payment. Repeat: This service *deserves* payment.

If you're tired of doing things in old ways, expecting different results that never happen, then you are ready to use your energy to accomplish goals that contribute to you and those you love. With as much honesty as you can muster, identify your fears and worries about money and being a reader; then take loving action in your own behalf so that you can overcome them. Go to therapy, if needed, so you can slay those dragons once and for all.

Drawing the Energy of Money to You

In your desire to serve and benefit others through your work as a professional tarot reader, a spiritual energy is called forth. You and this spirit cooperate fully as you use every bit of your creative talent to bring about good. In spite of any doubts about your abilities to pull it off, you say you will try to do your best. Allow yourself to imagine that you have the ability to succeed. We all do because the universe wants us to succeed. We were put here to be successful at life.

Sometimes, no matter how hard we try to realize our dreams, we run into stumbling blocks. The universe is limitless, but our ability to partake of its limitless bounty is determined by us, because our thoughts are real. Thoughts are actual realities that design the fabric of your experiences. Abundance is an outlook. Be generous and loving in your thoughts and actions about work, for as you are, your capacity to receive expands. Let your thoughts and actions be of divine awareness. Ask for money, then *expect* to receive it; if you expect nothing, you'll get what you expect. This law applies to all areas of your life.

I suggest that there are seven steps in drawing the energy of money to you: (1) become willing, (2) focus your intentions, (3) embrace your creativity, (4) set realistic goals, (5) ask for help, (6) let go of outcomes, and (7) say thank you with gratitude. Pull the following cards from your tarot deck: the Fool, the Magician, the Empress, the Emperor, the Star, the Hanged Man, and the World. Read the description of each, meditate, and make a journal entry about drawing the energy of money to you.

1. Become Willing (the Fool)

Being willing is the power to say "yes" in the midst of doubts, worries, and fears because you trust the process of discovery. It is a wake-up call to action and a leap of faith. Being willing to say "yes" is the key to creativity, power, and fulfillment because we realize that everything we find in our lives today is here to wake us up.

The true power of the Fool is unleashed when you say, "Yes, I'm willing to wake up to any area where I may have been asleep, including this one. Yes, I am willing to market and charge what I am worth. Yes, I am willing to recover some more or learn something new." Just knowing that you are willing to take a risk can be powerful and energizing. The more you operate from being willing, rather than from surface excuses and reasons to say "No, I can't," the greater the transformation you'll have with your relationship with money.

2. Focus Your Intentions (the Magician)

You currently possess all the strengths you need to draw the energy of money to you. Some are in full bloom, some are in seed form. How do you make your goal of being a successful professional tarot reader a reality? By focusing your intention on being a successful pro, you give direction, aim, and purpose to your goal that comes from deep within you.

Focused intention gives a clear, pure vision to energy and lives in the metaphysical realm. Intentions are more highly organized than ideas or wishes, closer to the laws of physics, and infinitely more powerful. You'll find both physical and mental rigor as you begin to focus your intention to draw money to you for the good of all. So, just like the Magician, now is the time to visualize your goal, focus your intention on abundance, and get to work.

3. Embrace Your Creativity (the Empress)

The Empress is the Great Mother who governs the cycles of work and play and grants us abundance. She represents creativity, good fortune, and success. Her domain is the emotions and intuition. Your openness, ability to nurture, and receptivity make you a good listener and excellent counselor. Ideas blossom and you know how to get the help you need because you are resourceful. By embracing the practical aspects of running a business through creative planning, prosperity finds you. Answers have a way of finding you, too. You have learned to nurture yourself and respect all that you are. You know that you are on your way to becoming all you can be.

4. Set Realistic Goals (the Emperor)

The problem with most goals is that they do not reflect what we really want out of life. Most of us don't distinguish between goals and tasks. They become as much fun as a "things to do" list. Get rid of "shoulda, coulda, woulda" on your list of realistic goals. These are *not* realistic goals because they are imposed by outside circumstances or worn-out beliefs. Goals that reflect your nature come from your heart and nurture your spirit. They express your life purpose and the intentions that lie at your core.

When you were a child you knew how to set goals that were creative and fun. As you got older, goals of this nature became the goals of "someday" or "one day" when life slowed down and you could finally dream again. We're happiest when we're creating a life we want and going out to get it. True goals, unlike the onerous "list of things to do," are meant to bring out a childlike excitement in you.

The Emperor draws his energy from fire and governs action and victory. Think about the work you most want and the goals that might take you there. Can you put your plan into action with the fiery passion of the Emperor?

5. Ask for Help (the Star)

Be open to intuitive guidance. Intuition means "inner teacher" and is the next logical step in the creative process of drawing the energy of money to you—the natural outcome of becoming willing, focusing your intention, and setting realistic goals. It is the predictable consequence of aligning your focused will with your heart's desire.

As we begin to control our minds, slay the dragons, and believe in ourselves, we awaken to the truth that we are spiritual beings. Divine guidance is always seeking to express itself through us. We become receptive to spiritual guidance in the form of using our psychic sense, connecting to our higher selves, and awakening to the God or Goddess of our understanding. This awakening turns our efforts into a series of synchronicities, psychic insights, and inspired solutions.

True spiritual guidance will direct your awareness to *solutions*, but asking for guidance requires a willingness to expect help. If we ask for help, but don't trust that it will come, we will get what we ask for. Expecting guidance is like adding an antenna to your psychic receiver, amplifying your receptivity. The Star is the inner light that guides us and offers spiritual gifts. Ask for help from the universe and expect to receive it.

6. Let Go of Outcomes (the Hanged Man)

You have created the circumstances for drawing the energy of money to you by being willing, focusing your intention, embracing creativity, setting realistic goals, and asking for help. Now it's time to let go of outcomes. Letting go instructs you to step aside and allow the universe to work its magic for a while. In other words, release your personal efforts to make things happen and put the process into the loving embrace of your Spiritual Source.

A gardener who hasn't planted seeds won't have a harvest. Nor will she if she doesn't tend to the weeding and feeding of her tender new sprouts. Yet, for all her work, it is the divine alchemy of the universe that causes the seed to grow. By planting and tending to your garden, you have set up the necessary conditions for the process to unfold. Just like the Hanged Man, when you allow things to happen without the need to control, the universe will orchestrate your magic and an abundant harvest is the natural outcome.

7. Say Thank You with Gratitude (the World)

The gateway to abundance is gratitude.[6] Abundance glows with the promise of "more," but "more" is not always a good goal. Amassing more stuff will not substitute for having clear goals that represent your heart's desire. Abundance is an appreciation of our life. We increase our power to attract the energy of money by embracing life's abundance—by saying "yes" to what life offers us, all of it, including scarcity. If we have never known scarcity, how can we appreciate abundance? We develop our ability to say "yes" to the energy of money by practicing gratitude for all the lessons that come our way.

So how can you be grateful for losing your job or having the electricity cut off? How do you wrap gratitude around that? Gratitude does *not* mean you jump for joy at life's misfortunes! It takes guts to live on this planet. Gratitude is a process of shifting the way you see events in your life so that you stay open to all the possibilities.

Gratitude allows you to receive the gifts of life, wherever and whenever they present themselves. When you receive gifts, you naturally want to give back. This maintains a flow of energy, a balance between giving and receiving. When you are balanced, you naturally open to the magic in your life. Your energy is free to create. You are open to possibilities, and you perceive your life as being blessed. You transmit this blessing to those around you and you are prosperous.

Just like the World suggests, you begin to realize that everything starts within and radiates outward. When you strike a balance between the physical and spiritual planes, you glimpse a deeper meaning of life's purpose. You are able to stand on solid ground inside yourself because abundance is not freedom from the storm, but equilibrium at its center. Success and fulfillment are yours because everything is available to you when your heart is full of gratitude.

You have now decided to take the leap of faith and start your journey as a professional tarot reader. Chapter 2 explores creative ways to build your practice. You begin by deciding what to charge for your time and expertise.

2 || Building Your Tarot Practice

Money will come when you are doing the right thing.

— Mike Phillips

In this chapter, you'll learn safety precautions when reading in the home and find creative places to read. By keeping a "tarot-to-go" kit ready, you'll never miss a spontaneous opportunity to make money when you encounter people who want readings on the spur of the moment.

You will also examine the difference between promotion and hype. "Getting the word out" about tarot services involves advertising. You'll explore the law of supply and demand and develop the skill of knowing what your clients need. Practical considerations include naming your business, low-cost ways to advertise, how to talk to clients about money, referring clients to another reader, and having a contingency plan for unexpected events. We begin by deciding what to charge for your services.

The $64,000 Question

What should you charge? Well, that depends on several things. Do you travel to a home or is your client coming to you? Are you a vendor, sharing part of your fee with a store owner? Do you read for entertainment at a party? Do you combine skills, such as a tarot reading with an astrological chart? Are you paying for table space at a psychic fair? Is there group pressure at a fair to charge the same fee? The guiding principle in all these questions is to be certain your fee structure reflects professional credibility. Never charge more than the market will bear because you will end up a very lonely tarot reader.

When you are starting out, there is a place for an apprenticeship period where you charge a smaller fee than the standard rate in order to introduce yourself and establish a clientele; but this can be a self-defeating practice in the long haul. It may be difficult to raise your rates once you charge too little and you become the victim of what I call the "ongoing sale" syndrome.

If you set a high price, I hope you are targeting a small market with no competition. Sound pricing strategy consists of setting your fee with the going rate for the industry. Call around. Ask what established professionals charge. When I was starting out, I charged the price of a good haircut. Right now, because of the counseling nature of my style and the years I've been at it, I charge what most psychologists charge: $100 per hour.

Decide first if you are charging for the reading or charging for your time. It is wiser to charge for your time, having a set rate for each fifteen-minute, half-hour, or hour-long reading. Early on, I found that charging for a reading, rather than charging for my time, was not a good business policy. If you charge per reading, you may end up receiving $30 for a ninety-minute marathon. I recommend that readings never go longer than sixty minutes because it is too exhausting. Collect fees at the beginning of a session. It is easier to disagree about price before a reading rather than after one.

Cash, Check, or Charge?

Once you have determined your fees, it's important to communicate the following to your clients: your basic session rate and duration of the session; alternatives such as longer sessions; options for other services, such as aromatherapy, massage, or astrological chart; and types of payment accepted such as cash, check, charge, or money order. You will also want to be clear on your refund policy and product guarantees.

Money orders are problematic because they suggest a predetermined fee and offer no room for spontaneous extended readings. As a vendor, decide which credit cards you will accept, then go to your bank and establish yourself as a vendor. You'll also need a machine to make credit card impressions. Your bank will help you with the details. Refer to chapter 3 for an in-depth look at merchant credit card accounts.

While credit cards make it easier for people to pay and make it easier for people to buy, credit terms are rare in professional tarot practice. It gets too messy. If a client forgets her checkbook, issue an IOU and send a friendly reminder in the mail two weeks later if she still hasn't paid.

If a client is experiencing cash-flow difficulties, consider using a sliding-scale fee. This can be awkward, however. It's tough to set one up in advance unless the client has said something while booking the appointment. If a sliding-scale fee comes out of your sincere desire to serve someone in financial misfortune, by all means do it. Be honest. Does charging less have anything to do with low self-worth? If so, don't do it.

If the fee is too low, you are going to be unhappy. Be sure you can live with the bottom of the scale because your clients will magically slide down to it. I do not recommend advertising a sliding-scale fee for obvious reasons. Suddenly, everyone qualifies! Carefully think through policies like sliding-scale fees. Having a "rescuer" motivation is a clue you shouldn't be doing it. It is best to take it on a case-by-case basis.

Bounced checks happen to the best of us, but as the recipient, you have to deal with the hassles. Consider charging a fee of at least $10 to $25 for bounced checks to cover your bank's charges and time involved in settling the account. Be aware that service charges can be contested if they aren't stated in your written policies. As a business, in most states you can go to the client's bank and get a preferential status in getting the check cashed as soon as funds are deposited into the account. I do not recommend any type of installment plan because, in my experience, I end up getting exactly what the client paid me at the end of the session and nothing more. Either decline the client's suggestion of an installment plan or consider a postdated check. I am old-fashioned. I deal almost exclusively in cold, hard cash, with the occasional check. I keep extra cash on hand in small denominations so that I can issue correct change.

Determining your fee involves more than deciding what to charge per hour. You have to balance desired income with expenses and what is realistic. You can be the best tarot reader in the world, but it is futile to charge more than the market will bear. Just because you desire a certain income doesn't mean people will pay it. Your fees must be fair and instill trust. Choose your market(s) carefully before you set your fees.

Raising Rates

Asking for more money can be a painful process in the helping fields. In other lines of work, for every year of experience you get a performance raise or cost-of-living salary increase. When you work for yourself, you also need to declare a periodic raise. Before you do, however, make certain your services are worth more than you now receive.

The first question to ask yourself is why you want more money. How long has it been since you've raised your rates? Find out if your income is comparable to your peers. Is your desire for more money based on need, performance, or reputation? Your financial needs and desires have nothing to do with your worth as a tarot reader. You deserve all the things you want in life, but your skills may not be as valuable in the eyes of your clients as you would like them to be.

Changing your fee too many times can look unstable or shady to your clients. When I started out I got stuck in the "ongoing sale" syndrome. In an effort to establish clients, I offered discounts until I dropped. I overloaded my clients with a plethora of options until nobody knew what I charged, including me! It got so my clients expected a deal of some sort and were miffed that I had the nerve to charge a straight fee. A possible timeline for raising your rates in a sane fashion is after three months for the first increase, no less than six months for the second hike, and no less than one year thereafter.

Like most people, we judge our worth partially on how much we make. If we charge more, we tend to think we're worth more. Not only will your clients take you more seriously and expect more, but you will too. You'll work harder after a fee increase. You will stretch yourself to be worth your new price. Because raising rates produces raised expectations, your readings will get better if you charge a little more.

Guarantees and Returns

Service and product guarantees instill client confidence. I recommend offering a money-back guarantee on all products and services. The first thing that clients see on my tarot class notebook is, "If, for any reason, you are not completely satisfied with this course, simply return all items within ten days of purchase for a 100 percent refund of materials and class fees. A satisfied customer is my best advertisement." Of course, to take a stand such as this, you need to carry quality products and deliver a fine service. It is wise to include a time limit on refunds, such as within ten days of purchase.

Speaking of refunds, always be ready to give a refund and offer an apology. Sometimes the cards don't cooperate or you're tired. Sometimes the chemistry between you and your client is all wrong. If a customer doesn't like your answer, don't change it to please her. Give a refund. It is better to lose your money than your integrity as a professional reader. *Never, never* argue with a client. Problem clients are more trouble than they're worth and you don't need the energy of *their* money in your life.

Talking to Clients About Fees

Ah, the heady moment has arrived. You're confident in your style and presentation, you've done your homework, you've set your fees, and now you're ready for your first paying customer. Enter reality. It is stressful to talk about what you charge. Salaried people with "real" jobs talk about it in an interview. Secretaries and receptionists handle the tacky transactions for psychologists. We tarot readers have to negotiate fees every time a potential customer calls.

Get comfortable saying your fee out loud. Practice in the shower. Tape it to the refrigerator. Repeat saying what you charge out loud every day. Have a friend ask you what you charge for a reading, look her straight in the eye and tell her. Go back and read the "Are You Funny About Money?" section in chapter 1.

So, the phone rings and the first thing you hear is, "What do you charge for a reading?" It may well feel like they are ready to accept or reject you based on one answer. You can respond with, "That depends on what you want." Then explore what they need based on the information found in chapter 5. If you have a menu of services with different prices, mention that too.

The second most frequently asked question after the fee is, "What does your fee include?" (Translation: "What am I getting for my money?") Potential clients are looking for "hidden" charges. Oh, she said she gave a twenty-five-minute reading for one set price, but she didn't bother to mention she charges extra for every minute after that!

I always include a tape of the reading as part of the fee and it seems to be a big selling point. For my tarot course, I give out a large notebook filled with useful information on the first night of class. It is included in the fee. I also have a frameable certificate of completion for my students and I write their names in calligraphy.

I am never in a hurry to make an appointment. I have a brochure that lists my prices and describes my services. I also include a "most frequently asked questions" sheet. When a new client calls, I suggest that I take her name and mailing information and send her a brochure and FAQ sheet. That way, she can look it over, find out more about my services, and decide if she likes what she sees. It saves lots of time on the phone. When she calls back, I know she is serious, or at least prepared to ask intelligent questions. If she calls back because she wants to argue with me, I politely hang up.

You can explain to a client what you do, but never justify what you do. There's a fine line between the two. For example, I tell my clients that an hour-long session is $100. They ask, "Why so much?" I explain in a professional voice that I combine two disciplines—tarot reading with energetic healing—and I do a careful health assessment first, so I provide a service that meets individual needs. I always end with, "I charge for my time and skill."

If I started justifying my fee, I might say something like, "Well, I'm the author of four books and I have been a registered nurse for twenty-five years and I've studied the tarot for longer than that." It not only destroys respect, but also conveys a lack of certainty that I'm worth it, or that I think a tad too highly of myself.

Justification also opens the door to client manipulation. Many callers want to bargain and don't feel they've done their job as a consumer unless they can get a few bucks knocked off the original price quote. Bargain hunting is a ritual with them. Just remember that a client's attempt at bargaining has nothing to do with your worth.

Some callers want a free sample reading. Some demonstration of your ability, such as a one-card interpretation, is not completely out of line if you feel comfortable with it; but people who demand a free reading before buying one rarely come in for a paying appointment. They are the same callers who want you to guess their astrological sign and divine what their great-grandmother's maiden name was. Hang up the phone.

The best solution is to offer references. Have a list of people who love your reading style and are willing to say so to a stranger. *Don't* give out your references' phone numbers or e-mail addresses. Rather, take your caller's phone number or e-mail address and have your reference contact the potential client. Or, have your reference put it in writing and keep copies to mail upon request. Again, omit the home address. It's sad but true: you never know who is on the other end of a call or e-mail. Be careful.

Ready, Set, Go

There are immediate opportunities to make money with the tarot cards and begin establishing yourself as a professional. The key to getting started is not so much staying up at night as being awake in the daytime. Pay attention!

One of the best ways to attract clients is to arrange to be a reader at a party or social gathering, where you do brief readings for a number of people in quick succession. This could be a fund-raising event, a psychic fair, or even a private party. Sometimes each client pays a small fee for the brief reading. (Be sure to bring change with you.) At a private party, the host or hostess usually pays a single, larger fee so the guests are not obliged. When I was starting out, I accepted donations and I labeled my little container "Good Karma Jar." My customers had smiles on their faces as they gave me money. Tricky psychology, huh?

Do you have a friend of a friend? Do you have a relative or friend expecting out-of-town guests? They might be willing to purchase a gift certificate from you. You can make the friend of a friend's visit memorable by giving her a tarot reading and leaving a tape. The gift certificate idea also works for birthdays, the holiday season, anniversaries, graduations, birth of a baby, or any other special life event. Generic gift certificates can be purchased in most office supply stores, or you can design your own on a home PC.

Local businesses with positive interest in psychic or New Age matters can be contacted as possible sources of clients. Call a yoga or health center, chiropractic office, herbal store, coffeehouse, psychotherapist's office, Universalist church, or metaphysical bookstore—anywhere at all your ideal client might be hiding. I do not read in bars because I have never found inebriation compatible with my purposes of healing. But I do know a woman who reads in bars and loves it. Different strokes for different folks.

If you are reading at someone else's business, be prepared to do a free reading with the owner, and maybe a staff member or two, as a way of interviewing you. Most businesspeople want to know who they are allowing into their work site. Don't take it as an insult. Their reputations, and therefore their livelihoods, depend on it.

Also clear up vending charges right away. Is the owner expecting part of your fee for the "rental" of her office space? Or does she feel that the reading is such a fine service that the attraction of more customers is payment enough? Will she actually charge you an hourly rental fee? Will you be considered a tarot reader on staff and receive a small fee for the extra business you bring in? I read at a university coffeehouse and all the owner requested was that each of my clients purchased a beverage before I read for them.

Be careful not to become the free help. I read at a New Age bookstore and was a vendor; that is, I paid the owner part of my fee for every client. She didn't pay me a dime. The more I read, the more money she made. Some days, business would be slow or I had a few moments before the next appointment. I knew something was amiss when she handed me the dust rag during one of those times. The owner didn't ask me, rather she *expected* me to dust her bookshelves, clean her bathrooms, tag her merchandise, and answer the phone when I wasn't reading—all without pay. Unless you are compensated for your work, do not become the janitorial service. You are a paid professional. Anything less is manipulation of your good nature and an issue of low self-esteem.

Freebie Advertising

Advertising is a necessity for starting your business. If you want to advertise immediately, consider your local community bulletin board for consumers. These can be found at grocery stores, coffeehouses, universities, and holistic health centers. Reality check: Remember that you are not advertising a mainstream service like pet sitting or childcare. Some local businesses with public bulletin boards will embrace your tarot service, some will not. Find your people and know who they are. If you have any doubt about the appropriateness of placing your ad, ask first.

Any local bulletin board or notice board that doesn't charge for display is a potential source of clients. Be sure your first flyer is attractive and looks professional. It is not a good idea to put your fees on a flyer and by all means, check the flyer for typos. I placed a flyer on an outdoor bulletin board near a university coffeehouse. Imagine how I felt when my creation disintegrated in the first rain. If your flyer will be exposed to the elements, weatherproof your display by laminating it. Any print shop can do this for a small fee.

I suggest you start with the basics of a flyer and business card. You can pay a printer for these services, but I created my own materials using nothing more than my home PC, Broderbund's Print Shop Deluxe, and my imagination. You can too, and save lots of money in the process. Are you flashy or mysterious? Do you prefer the bold or subtle approach? To get started, look at flyers and business cards that both repel and attract you. Fashion your own designs on what you learn from them and let your creativity shine.

I Need My Space

Okay, so you don't like to read in coffeehouses because they aren't private enough, you're tired of sharing your fee with the chiropractor, you can't stand the in-house bickering of the New Age bookstore staff, you're broke and can't afford to rent an office by the month or year, and the clatter of parties, street festivals, and psychic fairs destroys your concentration. What can you do? Plenty! Here are some alternatives:

- Find a suitable restaurant in an accessible location. Arrange to meet during quiet afternoon hours. Grab a back table or booth and order something. Don't stay longer than necessary and be sure to tip the server. You want to establish goodwill.

- Rent a small office *by the hour* from a psychotherapist who uses it mainly during the early morning and evening. Look in the yellow pages and start calling.

- Meet clients in *their* offices.

- Meet clients in public or college libraries. No, the atmosphere isn't "magical," but libraries often have private study rooms with doors.

- If the weather is good, meet clients in a safe park during daylight hours. Informal readings outdoors require only the space to sit on the ground and a cloth on which to lay your cards. Of course this doesn't work if the wind is strong enough to blow your cards away.

- Meet clients in your home.

- Meet clients in their home.

Please read on. Meeting clients in the home has some special considerations.

Mi Casa, Su Casa

I occasionally read tarot message boards. One day I saw the following two entries:

- "Avoid giving readings in your home or letting ANY of your clients know your home address or phone number. You never know who's going to become obsessed."

- "I read out of my home. I read at other people's homes. I did the storefront thing with a small New Age shop for four years. Thank you, I will read out of my home. My address is not listed in the phone book, just the phone number. I screen clients by phone call. If I am comfortable, they get the home address. If I am comfortable and circumstances warrant it, I will go to their home. Otherwise, I meet them at the local coffeehouse and read for them there. If I do go out on a call, I tell someone where I am going and about how long I will be there. I give my contact people the name and phone number of the client as well, and I have my pager with me at all times. It works for me, has for many years."

So, there you have it: never in the home; yes, in the home. How do you decide? Because of my familiarity with community health nursing, I picked up a few home safety tips[1] that I applied to reading in both my home and the homes of others. Safety should always be a concern for anyone in private practice. You don't always know who your clients are if they come to your office, rented space, or home, and you aren't always familiar with the neighborhood you'll be entering if you do on-site readings.

The following precautions are used when working in your home, rented space, or office; in other words, when clients are coming to you.

- Ideally, work hours only when someone else is in the building or your neighbor is home.

- If you are the only person in the building or your neighbor isn't home, call a friend *in the presence of your client* and tell your friend you will be calling after the appointment is over. This precaution also works when you are in someone else's home.

- Lock your door so uninvited people can't wander in. When I was renting an office, I always kept the door locked. I hung cheerful bells on the doorknob outside and the jingle was a pleasant way to announce my client's arrival.

- When working at night, make sure the area is well lit. Carry a whistle around your neck or on a key chain and don't be afraid to use it. Mischief-makers do not like noise.

- Keep your car in good condition and adequately fueled.

The following precautions are used when going to someone else's home; that is, when you are going to your client:

- Call your client ahead of time. Let him or her know when to expect you.

- Tell a trusted friend where you are going and when you'll return. Give your friend the client's name, address, and telephone number. Don't worry about confidentiality for safety's sake. You are not revealing the contents of the session.

- Take a map with you and make sure your car has gas.

- Schedule a first-time appointment for daylight hours only. If your client complains that he or she works, schedule the appointment for a day off. If the client doesn't want to do this and will meet only at night, do not make an appointment.

- Arrive early and survey the neighborhood. If it doesn't feel right, leave. Call your client and suggest meeting at a coffeehouse.

- If you have a cell phone or pager, take it with you. Make that call to a friend in the client's home within the client's hearing range. The cell phone is your link to the outside world and safety. Never hesitate to use it if you perceive danger or your car breaks down in an unknown neighborhood.

- If you sense that something doesn't feel quite right, trust it and leave! You have a right to stop a reading at any time for any reason.

I have read the cards for many years. In all that time, I can count on one hand how many clients have been menacing. Most clients are sincere in their search for answers. People operating from a lower frequency do exist, however. With a little common sense, trust-in-your-gut reactions to callers, and a few safety precautions, you can take your readings "on the road" and have a safe and prosperous tarot practice.

Tarot to Go

The telephone rings and one of your clients needs a reading about an important job interview that's coming up tomorrow. She requests an "emergency" reading. Can you come over right away? There is panic in her voice. It just so happens you have a block of free time. Now, where in the world are your deck, crystal, tape recorder, and cassettes?

If you want to read the cards professionally, you'd better get used to spur-of-the-moment calls. Most people don't plan ahead for a reading. The person who was cruising yesterday may perceive turmoil today, and clients want readings in times of indecision or doubt. I have never had a client request a reading because things were going too well.

You can avoid confusion and delays if you plan ahead and keep a "tarot-to-go" kit ready for spontaneous requests. To read for another, you need only your favorite deck of cards. For the professional reader, I suggest adding at least your business card, change if you expect cash payment, and a pen if the client pays by check.

Everyone must decide for themselves what should be included in a "tarot-to-go" kit. I have two versions. If I sense a client is not the least interested in atmosphere, I keep the following items ready to pick up and go: deck, business card, receipt book, pen, small denomination bills for change, a battery-operated tape recorder with batteries and cassette, a timer that I discreetly place toward me during the reading, a list of local counseling agencies, emergency phone numbers for when I'm in over my head, and Post-it Notes should I need to give my client such phone numbers.

If my client expects a certain ambiance, I also include: black velvet cloth, one large amethyst crystal, one clear quartz crystal, a purple votive candle and holder, incense burner and lighter, frankincense and myrrh or sandalwood incense, and a small trash bag with moist wipes to clean up any ashes.

All my accoutrements go in a black velvet bag. Desktop computer carryalls are about the right size. With just a little planning ahead, you'll be prepared for the spontaneity of professional tarot card reading. Keep a "tarot-to-go" kit ready and you'll always arrive cool, calm, and collected.

The Wind in Your Sales

I don't know about you, but the idea of promoting my tarot services is about as appealing to me as having a hangnail. At the risk of dating myself, selling something conjures images of door-to-door encyclopedia vendors, or used-car lots and guys named Johnny Fever. Tarot reading is supposed to be spiritual, darn it, and having to promote it feels cheap. If you, too, are uncomfortable with the idea of self-promotion, it helps to remember that you are not selling *yourself*, you are selling a *service*.

I define selling as the ability to make money on a regular basis by communicating persuasively with other people. If earning money with a deck of tarot cards is at the core of your career aspirations, you are in sales, like it or not.

In order to succeed in sales, you have to like serving people and getting paid to do it. If you like to serve people and money doesn't matter, become a volunteer. For your professional tarot practice to succeed, you need to observe what people want, communicate your ideas effectively, show passion for your services, and believe in yourself and what you're selling.

Business 101: The Law of Supply and Demand

You discovered the one-and-only you in chapter 1. After finding your niche as a professional reader, you must also ask your clients what they need and then become willing to supply it. Do your clients want relationship counseling, spiritual development, past-life or karma readings, career advice, health assessments, or tips on growing a business? Learn to be a specialist; that is, *supply* what the client wants or *demands*.

The law of supply and demand does not mean that you sell your soul for a buck. You never have to do anything repellant to you just because your clients want it. You honor the law of supply and demand by noticing the needs of others, and then you decide how you might fill their needs using your talents, experiences, and abilities.[2]

The "others" who need something are called a market. The most important business question you can ever ask yourself is, "What does the market *need* or *want* that I will *enjoy* providing?" If the market doesn't need or want it, and you don't enjoy offering it, your business venture will surely fail.

The marketplace has nothing to do with what we think people "should" want or need. Instead, the market is a place to observe people—what they want, need, and enjoy—and then do something creative with our observations. We need personal values because they guide us in our decisions, but it is not our job to "preach a right way" to anyone. We can best help people by noticing where they are, then creating a path or opening a door that is beneficial for both of us.

The law of supply and demand is a careful blending of your talents with the needs of others. It is not charging ahead with an idea that only you love. It is not giving up what you believe to be right to satisfy someone else. It is a perfect blend of your need to express your true self with your customer's need to have access to your skill, expertise, and creative talents and abilities.

You identified your unique selling points (your niche) in chapter 1. Now translate your ideas into a thirty-word statement of what your tarot service will do: "My tarot business will . . ."

Certainly you can charge ahead unprepared and hope for the best. But then you won't be any different from a lot of other readers barely making ends meet. I believe that many gifted readers are financially struggling, not because they lack skill or a caring heart, but because they haven't thought the whole venture through, haven't identified a target market, and haven't marketed the talents and abilities that set them apart from the pack. Understanding the law of supply and demand will help you do just that.

Testing the Waters

Before you quit your job, spend lots of money on professional brochures, and open your new tarot enterprise, take these steps to determine if professional tarot reading will succeed in your area:

1. Try reading the cards on a part-time basis to get a sense of what attracts people and how much they are willing to pay for your service. Read at psychic fairs, bookstores, street festivals, chiropractic offices, yoga centers, anywhere your ideal client might be found.

2. Work for an established business that offers tarot readings such as a bookstore or coffeehouse. Work there long enough to see what is truly involved on a regular basis when reading the cards for money. Is this something you really want to do every day? People without problems rarely want a reading. Do you like interacting with people who have problems well enough to make tarot reading a career?

3. Rent a booth at a community festival, block party, or psychic fair. Chat at length with anyone who stops to talk or ask questions, and eavesdrop on comments of people who walk by. Are there enough people in your geographic area to support your reading services? Were you ignored or ridiculed? (There's a clue.) Or were you busy, with lines forming around you? In short, did people accept or reject your services?

4. Get to know other readers in your community. Go through the yellow pages or look at community bulletin boards to find established readers. Call or visit as many of them as you can. Pay for as many professional readings as you can afford and note their style of presentation. Pick their brains. Be open about what you are doing. Professional readers know that studying the "competition" is standard business practice. There is room enough for everyone and most are willing to share success tips. If an established reader is unwilling to help you, cross her off your list of referrals because you don't need her energy in your life. The value of making referrals is covered at the end of this chapter.

5. Call the Chamber of Commerce or Small Business Administration to get marketplace data from your geographic area. The Chamber

of Commerce or Small Business Administration carefully monitors the economic pulse of their communities. They know what types of businesses are opening or closing and what types of consumers are moving in or out. Red lights should flash for you if a New Age business such as a healing touch center, herbal supply company, or bookstore just went under in your area. Call the former owners of such businesses, if possible. Try to establish the reasons for business closings before you share the same fate.

Do the preliminary work suggested above while you still have your day job. Ease your way into your new life as a full-time tarot reader because success doesn't happen overnight. One golden rule of business is that cash will come in more slowly and go out more quickly than you expect.[3] Never count on money you haven't earned yet.

Remember that geographic areas are different. Some communities will embrace you while others will want to burn you at the stake. Spend an hour every night on necessary reading or planning that moves you closer to your career goals. When you're ready to experiment with your plan, take a part-time job to keep guaranteed money flowing while you test the waters for success.

What's in a Name?

Selecting company names is big business in America and plenty of high-priced consulting firms prove it. You don't need an ad agency to choose your tarot business name, but it does require careful thought. Some fields, like law, traditionally use the last names of the partners. How bland. The artistic, intuitive field of tarot reading invites creativity. Choosing a name for your tarot service is a pleasant task and it makes it easier to visualize the business. When you name your tarot practice, somehow the entire start-up process feels more real.

Finding the perfect name for your tarot business is an important task. The name you choose will position you in people's minds, affect the image you project, and have a major impact on your success.

The costs of a poor name, and therefore poor advertising, are extravagant. Putting out the wrong message or the wrong image for your tarot business costs immediate dollars, but the opportunity cost of lost sales is tremendous. Make sure you start out on the right foot. Your tarot business name needs to be functional, clear, appealing, and descriptive. What exactly does a business called "The Left-Handed Moon" offer? It is wise to avoid nebulous names. You want a positive image that you can display with confidence and pride.

So how do you find the perfect name for your tarot reading service? There are two kinds of advice: professional advisors, such as the folks who work at ad agencies; and informal advisors, other tarot readers, family, and friends. Program a dream for several nights in a row, ask the tarot cards to give you a name, meditate, brainstorm, free-associate, do a naming ritual or spell. Ask for help from family and friends but rely on your own intuition for the final decision. It's *your* business after all.

Try your business name out on people who don't know you and your tarot business idea. Go to a friendly place like a New Age bookstore and ask the owners and employees what they think of your business name. Let them react to only your name, which is exactly the way a potential customer would react to your phone listing, business card, or flyer.

Explain that you are trying it on for size and ask what they think of it. What does the name convey? Everyone likes to offer opinions. You might also find a customer or two willing to participate. Of course, you don't have to accept anyone's advice, but you could get constructive criticism, wonderful positive feedback, and fresh, new ideas.

Don't choose the first name that comes to you. Make a list, ask your friends, cruise the yellow pages—not just in your area, but other places too. Maybe your selection is taken. You don't want to find this out after you have spent time and money on business cards, flyers, brochures, signs, stationery, and listed your business in the phone book.

Choose more than one name for your tarot business. You can't use a name that belongs to another business. If you plan to operate under your own legal name, no registration is required. Today, with an increasing number of metaphysical businesses and the Internet, some names are trademarked and off limits for use by others. By having several name choices, if your first choice is not available, you'll be ready with other options. The easiest way to check names already taken in your area is to look in the yellow pages first. It takes a few more complicated steps to check for trademarks and register your own business name, but it is well worth the effort. The following guidelines will help you with your name registration:[4]

- Begin your free trademark search online at www.nameprotect. com. You can also go directly to the U.S. Patent and Trademark Office at http://patents.uspto.gov/main/trademarks.htm. If you do not have access to a computer, try the local library or your city's register of deeds. They both carry registered trademark information but a small fee is required to do the search. Domain name registration is covered in chapter 3.

- Registration of a business name varies from state to state. It takes a few phone calls to discover the registration process in any state. Using the blue pages of your telephone book, start by calling the county clerk or the information number of the county executive office. Someone there can direct you to the registration process specific to your state. You might also be able to register your name by going to the register of deeds office in your city. Call first to avoid a wild goose chase. There will be a nominal fee for registration.

A Picture Is Worth a Thousand Words

Having a logo for your tarot business isn't essential, but an attractive graphic adds visual interest to your business cards, flyers, and brochures. It becomes your trademark whether you register it or not. If you decide to use a logo, remember that it is as powerful in its image projection as your name, maybe more so, because people tend to look at pictures before they read the words. Choose your logo carefully.

If you want a logo for your tarot reading service, decide upon one in the beginning so you can register your name and logo at the same time. It also costs less to have your logo printed on your company materials such as business cards, brochures, and stationery at the outset, rather than trying to piecemeal it together later.[5]

If you like to work with computers, many software programs offer clip art for the public domain. In other words, the clip art is intended for home, school, and small business use. Be aware that, while you can "borrow" a clip art graphic to use as your logo, you cannot register it as your own. The copyright still belongs to the software company that produced it, such as Broderbund. If you want to register your logo, consider hiring an art student or aspiring artist to design an original logo for you. Call the local art school, place a notice on the school's employment bulletin board, or run a "help wanted" classified ad in your local newspaper.

Be aware of copyright and trademark law when designing a logo. You cannot copy something from a book or magazine just because you like it. Almost everyone with basic computer skills knows they can right-click on any online graphic and copy it for personal use. This is a very bad (and illegal) idea. While the Internet may be the "World-Wide Copy Machine," all copyright laws apply to it. It is unethical to rip-off an online graphic because we know we can get away with it. Choose wisely.

Think hard before you choose the skull and crossbones, spiders, bats, or a raven's claw as your logo. Your selection may be trendy or laden with symbolism to many people, but you may also be scaring away a lot of potential customers. The average person lacks insider knowledge of New Age symbols and hasn't a clue about the significance of Grandmother Spider. All she knows is that she is terrified of spiders. For the sake of expanding your business, don't frighten people with your logo.

Advertising

Getting the word out about your tarot services involves advertising. After all, people need to know you exist, but let's explore the difference between promotion and hype. Look at any New Age paper or magazine and scan through the ads. Notice which ones make you feel like calling them on the spot. If you keep reading ads, you'll develop a sense of what is genuine. Model your ads and promotional materials on the ones that make you want to call.

The biggest mistakes that tarot readers make, in my opinion, are exaggeration, overuse of uppercase letters, and too many exclamation points. I recently saw this ad: "EXTREMELY GIFTED PSYCHIC! MY READING WILL CHANGE YOUR LIFE! CALL ME TODAY!" Extremely gifted? As opposed to what? Slightly gifted? One reading will change my life? Please. And what's with the capitalization and exclamation points? I felt like the advertiser was shouting at me.

People despise being hustled. You want to promote yourself without going overboard into hype. Spiritual hype is repulsive. Never promise something you can't deliver and don't exaggerate your skill. Remember that your clients will know when you are hustling them. They will also know when you are trying to help them. So how can you promote yourself without crossing the line into hype? It's simple: Never claim to do what you cannot do. People will respect your honesty most of all.

Put Customers First

From my experience, people decide whether or not to buy my services in less than a minute. I don't have long to explain my value. Whether making contact by phone, e-mail, face-to-face at a booth, or through advertisements, put potential customers first by finding out what they need from you right away. Spend most of your time or ad space explaining what you can *do* for a client.

Only after people understand that what you offer is valuable to them, are they ready to hear how qualified you are. Sell yourself after you have sold the need for your services. Mention your credentials, of course, but don't launch into a personal admiration party. Any potential client will lose interest fast if you talk too much about the wonders of you. The best advertisement for your work is a quality reading.

What you have to sell is much the same as every other tarot reader in the eyes of the person reading the ad. But you know you are different, and your ad must reflect it. If you want to learn how to write killer ads in a short period of time, I recommend *The Copywriter's Handbook: A Step-by-Step Guide to Writing Copy That Sells* by Robert W. Bly (Henry Holt and Company, 1990). Be sure to include a headline that draws attention to your ad, a brief explanation of your services, and your name and contact information.[6]

Where to Advertise

The basic task of effective advertising is to pinpoint the need you are meeting and answer one question: Exactly what problem do you solve? If you're off base with ineffective advertising, your income falls. Examples of ineffective advertising include distributing your literature to the wrong people, placing ads in the wrong newspaper, placing ads at the wrong time, or advertising the wrong services for the target market in your area.[7]

Buying ad space is always a risk because it may or may not work. Ad space is expensive. Will you get one hundred responses or none for your investment? It depends on whether or not the publication reaches your most likely clients and whether or not your ad attracts them.

Before placing an ad in a magazine or newspaper, consider who reads it, how many read it, and where they are located. Will the ad appear daily, weekly, monthly, or quarterly? Make sure you can afford to invest in advertising because you may not get a return on your money.

Most ads do not bring in immediate business. If you run an ad only once, don't wonder why no one called. A person reading your ad may not need your services at the time and assume you'll advertise again. If your ad disappears, that person will assume you have disappeared too.

Check to see if other tarot readers are advertising in the local newspaper. It usually indicates whether or not they are getting business through the classifieds. To be candid, newspapers are not where people usually look to find a tarot reader. People do read local New Age publications for the ads placed by astrologers, hands-on healers, tarot readers, and the like.

Advertising on the radio and television is more expensive than the average tarot reader can afford, but check out any small local radio or television station because they may be within your budget. Never underestimate the power of radio or television to reach thousands of potential customers.[8]

Whatever Goes Around Comes Around

Suppose someone calls and asks you for a health-related reading. If you don't know an antigen from an antibody, say so, and refer the person to someone who does. Stay focused on your client's needs and not on your ego. It's not your session. You are making a living because someone is paying you for a service that you can provide. If you can't provide it, suggest someone who can. Establishing goodwill in the community is called networking and can greatly expand your business.

Seek out people who can refer customers to you. Look for professionals in related fields and introduce yourself. I make a point of knowing people whose clientele are similar to mine. For example, I know several astrologers. Because I do health-related readings, I also have valuable contacts with massage therapists. Please note: Referrals are meant to be reciprocal so that both parties can benefit.

Referrals can come from unexpected places. Don't forget to tell your neighbors, classmates, former coworkers, and relatives about your new business. The more people know what services you offer, the more likely you are to get recommendations.[9]

Tarot reading is a rewarding profession but you are human and stuff happens. What if you or your child gets sick? Breaking appointments is the surest way to lose customers. Consider having another reader as official backup. Do the same for her. You can substitute for each other in a crunch, or when one of you desperately needs a vacation. Work out a method of payment in advance to avoid misunderstandings later.[10]

You have explored the nuts and bolts of starting a professional tarot service. Chapter 3 broadens the horizon as you take a leap into cyberspace.

3 ‖ Global Tarot

*Whatever you think you can do, or dream you can,
begin it.*
   Boldness has genius, magic and power in it.

— Goethe

In this chapter, you will explore phone consultations and having a
tarot practice in cyberspace. You'll also learn tricks of the trade from
Diane Wilkes, web mistress of TarotPassages.com, the best tarot site
on the Internet today.

Are you ready for the World Wide Web? It's as simple or complicated
as you want it to be. Computer technology is constantly changing.
Today's marvel is tomorrow's relic. Websites, e-mail lists, and chat rooms
come and go. For these reasons, chapter 3 doesn't cover the specifics of
website design, Internet advertising, custom design versus predesigned
websites, Internet service providers (ISPs), learning hypertext markup
language (HTML), selecting graphics, using bulletin boards, signing on
to e-mail lists, or participating in tarot chat rooms. Instead, you will find
general pointers that serve as a "broad overview" to get you started.

You have many options for finding specific "how to" information
including: the use of a search engine such as Go.com to locate fellow
tarot enthusiasts; do-it-yourself HTML manuals; community web-
design classes; using a server with a predesigned page (no required

knowledge of HTML); buying website-creation software such as Dreamweaver; or hiring a professional web designer, the most costly method. For a realistic idea of what is involved and making an informed decision based on it, please refer to appendix C for learning resources that are up-to-date at press time.

My own website is a combination: a predesigned page, but because I know a little HTML code, I can customize it by adding links and targets. I started on my own by reading books on the subject. Then I took a noncredit web design course at the local university and asked lots of questions.

Web design programs, such as those produced by Adobe, are expensive, take mega amounts of hard disk space, and you need a fast computer, but you have unlimited creativity in return. Many web design programs, such as FrontPage, do not require HTML code knowledge and you can use them if you know how to use Windows.

My website is browser based, meaning I do not have to download tons of software to my hard drive or know file transfer protocol (FTP). My server does all the work for me. The drawbacks are many, such as few creative choices in layout or design, limited space for graphics, and no tracking of visitors. But for $30 a year and my time, I have a serviceable site that I can modify at any time. Since writing this chapter, I have upgraded my website. I still have browser-based software with all its advantages and drawbacks, but for $150 a year, I now have ten pages, room for many graphics, and a traffic meter. Plan your website based on your needs before you take the plunge: the fancier and bigger it is, the more it will cost.

The World Wide Web

If you decide to have a website, the first thing you want to do is register a domain name. A domain name is a unique name that identifies a site on the Internet.[1] You want to select and register a name that describes your business. Your domain name should be easy to spell, describe your business, and be memorable.

Once you decide on a name, the next step is to register it. In the beginning, domain names were registered by one company called Network Solutions. In 1999, Network Solutions lost its exclusive right to register domain names, so today many other companies offer registration services. You also need to submit your registered domain name to large search engines such as Yahoo.com to increase traffic flow.

There can be fees for everything from registration service to site hosting to submitting your site to search engines. See what each company offers and where the hidden charges lie. In order to determine the value of a company's service, simply compare the total cost to the services offered. Look around before choosing a company because prices vary.

When designing a web page, ask yourself what you want your site to do for you and your clients. Before charging into anything, describe your site in plain English. How do you want it to look? How will the look relate to what you want to do; namely, read the tarot cards? How much time and money are you willing to spend on website design and maintenance?

Remember that a site must have good content and be free of grammatical errors or it is useless to your visitors. It should be easy to use and well organized, while holding your visitor's attention until your message has been communicated. The biggest mistake people make in web design is having too many cutesy, animated graphics popping up all over the place. It's irritating and causes headache. Avoid hard-to-read colors, glaring backgrounds, or fancy fonts that are too small to read without eyestrain. Have a clear table of contents no larger than one screen, and make your page easy to navigate. Use lots of space between topics. Above all, concentrate on your message. Yes, your web page needs to be easy on the eyes, organized, and a breeze to navigate, but content (your message), not looks, is what counts in the long run.[2]

As obvious as this may appear, you need to know what you want your site to achieve. Plan before you build. Have specific goals and review them often. Design your site for your client, not for yourself. It is your quality service, not the wonders of you, that is going to get people to spend hard-earned money. Put the focus on your services and your clients' needs, and save the self-promotion for the "About Me" page. It costs money to maintain a website. Make sure it is in your budget. The web is different from all your other marketing efforts. It is not television or print media. The content for a website should be developed specifically for the website.[3]

You have already looked at the importance of having a secure site for payment by credit card. It is a good idea to guarantee privacy. Clients are concerned about privacy and security on the Internet. If you plan to read the cards on the web, accept credit card payment, provide electronic cash options, or sell merchandise, it is important to explain to your clients how you handle online security and why their information is safe.

Besides having the right security technology in place and feeling safe yourself, you want your clients to feel safe too. You'll encourage online buying, as well as head off complaints later, if you explain your security measures in plain English at your site. A security policy should be in place with a link to a copy of that policy.[4]

A word about e-mail: E-mail is one of the oldest technologies on the Internet and is useful in soliciting new customers and providing information or customer service. While you can think of it as a form of electronic direct-mail marketing, there are some rules to follow.

No one likes to be bombarded by mail they did not solicit. Junk mail on the Internet is called spam.[5] You can target your e-mail market by advertising a mailing list on your site that people voluntarily join. They choose to be on your mailing list. Remember, too, that they can choose to be taken off your list and you must respect the request.

You can also rent a list of potential customers from a list rental service. The cost per thousand addresses is currently between $150 and $200. Remember that the idea behind e-mail lists is *direct* marketing, not mass marketing. People voluntarily subscribe to "opt in" e-mail lists. They may also "opt out." The company from which you rent should use verification procedures to make certain everyone is on the list of their own free will.[6]

Not all list providers are ethical. Many have huge lists comprised of people who did not join. Please don't risk your reputation by sending this kind of unsolicited e-mail. People do not like spam. But how did unethical list providers get the names? There are as many ways to hack e-mail addresses as there are hackers.

Anytime you buy online, the vendor may sell your e-mail address to similar businesses. Your Internet service provider or website host may also sell your address to list servers. Read all company privacy policies before you purchase anything and ask that your e-mail address not be sold or given away. Every time we send or receive a forwarded message, we have placed our e-mail address in cyberspace, especially if our address is in the carbon copy or CC field. It becomes fair game to anyone in a position to retrieve it. The easiest way to reduce spam is for us to stop forwarding our own junk.

According to the Coalition Against Unsolicited Commercial E-mail (www.cauce.org), it is ineffective to click the "Remove from list" link on most spam correspondence. Why? Because it serves to only confirm your e-mail address! We end up getting more junk mail. CAUCE suggests one trick to stop spam that works above all others: Don't open junk e-mail and permanently delete it. That's it! It takes a few minutes (or seconds) once a day. In so doing, I have reduced my spam titer by two-thirds. It works. Really.

Protect your clients as you would want to be protected. Never sell your e-mail list to anyone for any reason. Take steps to keep your clients' e-mail addresses private. You will lose good repeat and word-of-mouth customers when they discover how their names got all over the Internet. Don't write your recipient's address in the carbon copy or CC field. If you do, all recipients will see all addresses. You might not sell your list but that doesn't mean someone else won't. Your clients are gold. Treat them that way.

E-mail marketing is a type of advertising too. You wouldn't post an ad without first proofreading it, would you? You should also proofread any direct e-mail you are sending. Use the spell checker and make sure you are spelling your client's name correctly. Nothing screams "amateur" louder than an e-mail filled with the grammatical errors of a sixth-grader or too many exclamation points. Exclamation points look like shouting. For an excellent online guide, please visit "How to Write E-mail Ads" at www.findmorebuyers.com/page.cfm/198.

Periodically clean up your e-mail list to keep it current. And finally, avoid sending e-mail with attached files. Executable, attached files are the most common way viruses are spread over the Internet. If your announcement comes in the form of an attached file, virus-conscious clients may delete the e-mail without reading it. (I do without exception.) If you feel you must attach a file, be sure to confirm that your client has the capability to download an attachment without crashing and that the program you used to create the file is compatible with their software. Bottom line: Make life easier for everyone by avoiding attachments altogether.

Method of Payment

Whether reading by phone or electronically, the same rule applies: When the reading isn't done face-to-face, decide *first* how you will collect the payment, issue refunds, and deal with nonpayment.

Will you accept cash, electronic cash, check, money order, or credit card? Will you collect fees before or after the reading? What is your plan if you collect payment after a reading and clients either don't pay or the check bounces? How will you issue a refund to an unsatisfied customer? What happens when the cards don't cooperate and you can't read? Answer all of these questions upfront to avoid misunderstandings later.

Here's how I organize phone consultation payment, and keep in mind this is one woman's method (you can find more ideas in appendix C): A client contacts me for a phone consultation. I quote my price and tell her I will call back with appointment times when I receive her check or money order. I never accept cash through the mail. If my follow-up is a toll call, I inform the client that the call will be collect.

When I receive payment and the check clears, I call her with a few appointment times. We select one. On the day of the appointment, my client calls me at the scheduled time and we proceed. If she is late call-ing, or misses the consultation altogether, I give her one more chance to reschedule, and inform her that if she misses another appointment without twenty-four-hour advance notice, I keep the fee. I do this to avoid being at the mercy of someone else's agenda.

If this sounds like a hard-line policy to you, please remember that you are a professional and your time is as valuable as any other pro-fessional. Would a psychotherapist or counselor expect anything less? You shouldn't either.

Whether or not you offer your client the option of paying for a phone reading with a credit card is up to you. You'll need to set up a merchant account at your bank and the setup fees can range from $25 to $250. The bank's charges on gross sales may be hefty. You may have to pay a fee every time you call in a charge, there can be a week's delay in accessing the money, and the client has up to six months to refute the charge. If you operate a home business you may find it hard to get a merchant account, but check the yellow pages under "Credit Cards"; some credit card companies issue merchant numbers and credit card plates.[7]

I personally see this as too much of a hassle, but credit cards are easy for your client to use. They also encourage larger purchases than buying without credit and make out-of-state or gift certificate read-ings more convenient. If you sell products such as herbs, crystals, or astrology charts along with your readings, or teach a class, credit cards are probably the way to go.

A few words about payments in cyberspace: Internet payment meth-ods are evolving. A few years ago, telephone transactions were suspect. Now they are big business and banks have worked out their policies for them. As e-commerce grows, banks will also fine-tune online payment methods, but for now there are a few kinks.

I visited a large bank in my area to learn how to accept credit cards online. Here is what I gathered: At the time of this writing, you must first have a "card not present" (or CNP) merchant credit card account.[8] "Card not present" literally means you do not see the customer or the card during the transaction, so the interchange carries risk.

The most interesting thing I learned is that for a bank, online credit card transactions are a matter of assessing—and paying for—risk. The riskier your business is perceived by the credit card company and bank, the higher your fees will be to accept credit card payments. And yes, professional tarot reading is seen as a high-risk category at this bank. Take comfort in knowing that *any* new business is considered high risk at the start, and a good track record may slowly lower your fees. Because banks vary on their philosophy of risk, check out several and compare before setting up shop.

Please note, too, that once you open a CNP account so you can accept credit cards online, you then need to get a secure website. (You know, the one that has a little padlock icon in the corner.) There is a whole array of products that allows you to set up a secure site ranging from the simple to the complex. Building a secure site is not within the scope of this book, but you can research online for service and software product solutions. Look in appendix C for books about business on the web.

Most clients look for secure sites and will not purchase from an unprotected vendor. Hackers are not after *one* credit card. They want the site where lots of credit card information is stored. Make sure your customer's information is secure.

Electronic cash, such as CyberCoin, is a newer form of online payment. For it to work, both you and your client have to participate in the system. You have to accept electronic cash and your client has to establish an electronic account. The customer advances cash into an "electronic wallet" from his or her checking account or credit card advance. Once the money is deposited into an electronic cash account, it's simply a matter of paying via this account to any merchant who accepts it. (That would be you.)

No money moves online because the money never leaves the banking system. It is deposited from your customer's electronic cash account into yours. Credit cards are still the most common means of purchasing on the web, and electronic cash companies have not yet taken the Internet by storm.[9] Use a large search engine, such as Yahoo.com or Lycos.com, to find information on electronic cash companies. Then decide if it's the method for you.

Telephone Etiquette

Okay, you've determined a method of payment and collection and you've worked out your refund policy. The telephone rings. Now what do you do? The telephone plays a vital role in your business. Clients call to get information about your services and to book appointments. Telephone etiquette is important because it may be the first impression a potential buyer has about you and your tarot reading. Here are some pointers:[10]

- Answer the phone quickly, after two rings if possible.

- Identify yourself and include the name of your tarot service, if you have one.

- Speak in a friendly, courteous, and confident tone. (It may sound silly, but smile as you speak. Smiling is reflected in the tone of your voice.)

- Do *not* put the caller on hold, if at all possible! It is rude. If you must place the caller on hold, get back within one minute or you have lost the call. Be sure to say, "Thank you for waiting."

- Remember that the person called you because she wants to understand your services. Either take the caller's address and mail a FAQ sheet with a brochure or be willing to patiently answer your client's questions. (I prefer the first method because it saves time.) It is natural for a new client to have some questions about the quality of your readings.

- Use the phone to quickly assess client expectations. If you can't provide the service, refer the caller to someone who can. Your goodwill and honesty will be remembered.

- When using an answering machine, personalize it with your name and the name of your reading service; keep it brief, and say when customer calls are returned.

- Please, please, please do not allow children to answer your business calls or record your message. You may think it's cute, but nothing takes the "professional" out of tarot reader faster than children babbling into the phone.

- Return all calls promptly; the sooner, the better!

- When you're starting out, keep a written script (narrative) about your services beside the phone. Referring to the script will keep you from rambling.

- Sharpen your skills by practicing your script in front of the mirror or with a friend. Anticipate questions and write scripts for those too. The importance of telephone skills in a service business cannot be overemphasized.

Getting Connected

Some readers hire an answering service if it is within their budget because it adds a personal touch and it appears professional. Calls are forwarded to the company they've hired and a real live person answers their calls and takes messages. These readers simply call the service to retrieve messages.

I personally do not use an answering service because the operators are not qualified, authorized, or paid to offer specific information about my readings. Clients call because they want help now. Potential clients may become frustrated when they reach a person who can't do anything more than take a message. Plus, answering services can be expensive. If this is the way you want to go, shop around because prices and services do vary.

When answering machines first came upon the scene, everyone hated them and many people refused to leave a message. Because they are now commonplace, we have become accustomed to talking to a machine. In fact, I am startled when a real person picks up the phone.

While answering machines are inexpensive, you may also want to consider voice mail. Find out what types of voice mail services are available through your local telephone company and compare prices to independent communications companies. Another option is computer software that gives callers a menu of options, such as "Press 1 if you want to receive a brochure, press 2 if you want to schedule an appointment," and so on. Menus are impressive, but they may be more than you need when starting out.

With answering machines and voice mail, you have the advantage of customizing your message to fit your business needs. For example, are you offering any introductory specials, going on vacation, appearing at a psychic festival, closed for personal reasons, accepting new clients, changing your hours, adding a service or product, celebrating a holiday with a package deal, or moving? Of course, answering machines can malfunction because the electricity goes off or you run out of tape, but events like these don't happen often, especially if you check your messages every day. Voice mail rarely malfunctions, but ask about the risks associated with this system before buying it.

Whatever system you choose, please keep your message professional because first impressions are lasting ones. Make your greeting pleasant. Do what you say you will do: State when callers can expect a return call and meet that expectation.

Cell phones are wonderful inventions when you consider how handy they are for conducting business and promptly returning your messages. Plus, they provide extra security. After 9/11, no one can deny the value of a cellular phone. The prices have come down and there is a cell phone to fit every budget.

Knowing that help is only a phone call away is reassuring when you're driving into an unfamiliar neighborhood, entering a home for a first-time reading, having car trouble, in need of calling the psychiatric emergency room because your client's problems are beyond the scope of a reading, or running late for an appointment. Please remember courtesy and driving safety when using a cell phone.

Another communication option is the personal pager. Callers can let you know when they wish to speak to you. Pagers can be time-savers. For instance, receiving word about a last-minute cancellation could prevent an unnecessary trip to a client's home. I don't have a pager for two reasons: Getting to a phone to answer a page is frustrating and I feel like a puppet on a string; and two, I don't want to be accessible to my clients twenty-four hours a day because of boundary issues. Before you advertise your pager number, ask yourself one question: Do you really want to be reachable at all hours of the day or night?

Telephone Tarot

How you set up your reading space, prepare for phone consultations, contact your spirit guides, choose a deck, clear the cards, select a layout, or protect yourself from negative energy is up to you. Refer to appendix A for one version of a tarot reader's code of ethics. appendix C has resources for learning more about 900-telephone-line reading companies. Here are some general tips that I have learned over the years:

- By law, your caller must be eighteen years old to purchase a reading. If you suspect your caller is a minor, say so, and politely hang up the phone. Better to be safe than sorry.

- Do your preliminary work ahead of time. Make certain your caller understands exactly what you can and cannot do before the reading begins. See why the FAQ sheet or brochure from chapter 2 is so important?

- Keep your focus on the caller. If astrological information is helpful to you, ask for the caller's birth date. Clarify whether it is to be a general or specific reading. I start by asking my Spiritual Source to help me provide information in the most understandable form possible, covering what is needed now for the highest good of all. I also remind the caller that the reading belongs to her. She is free to ask questions or add insights at any time.

- Listen very carefully to your caller so you can sense when she wants to discuss something in greater detail, or when you are overloading her with too much information. Even if the solution to someone's problem looks crystal clear to you, it is not your place to judge readiness. The reading belongs to your caller. Let it go where it needs to go for the highest good of your client.

- Watch the time! Start summing up during the last ten minutes. With about five minutes left, ask your caller if there are any final comments or questions.

- Give your caller the chance to hang up first. From my experience, clients don't like to feel that I have hung up on them, especially if the reading was difficult. Of course, if the time is up, and you have a chatterbox on the other end, you can say, "Our time is up now. Thank you very much for calling. Best wishes to you." Then hang up the phone.

Heavy-Duty Cards

Your job is to be honest, helpful, and supportive. Try to remember that every card presents an opportunity to learn and grow. Challenges make us strong. The cards may not tell us what we want to know but they will reveal what we need to know. Never predict physical death or catastrophe. We don't have that kind of power and we have no right to take away someone else's hope. Everyone can change outcomes, at least to some degree, by changing attitudes and behavior.

When you see death or an accident, remind the caller to take very good care of herself. You can say anything that points her in the right direction: Be extra careful today, get your brakes checked, see your doctor for a checkup, you are entering a time of letting go—anything that gives the power of choice back to your caller so she can face the events in her life and make changes with courage.

If the cards are truly mind-boggling, look at one card at a time, then see what significance it holds to the rest of the layout. Break the reading into small bits of information. Ask lots of questions. Find a way to gently point your client toward the truth without bludgeoning her over the head with it or scaring her to death. And don't forget to breathe deeply for relaxation throughout a difficult reading.

Sticky Situations

Whether you're just starting out or you've been reading by phone for years, every reader runs into unpleasant callers. I have found that having my callers pay first is a great way to decrease the risk of nastiness. People rarely want to pay for being a jerk! But, you have advertised and your phone number is on the business cards you left at the coffeehouse. No matter how careful you are, stuff happens. It's the nature of the business. What'cha gonna do? Here are a few guidelines:

- *Obscene callers and drunks:* For callers using sexually explicit language or those with slurred speech, tell them they have the wrong phone number and hang up. If they call back, pull your telephone plug for a while. If it persists, report it to your phone company. The phone book carries information about telephone harassment.

- *Verbal abuse:* I've had people call and tell me I am doing the devil's work. If someone calls to inform you of your "scam," hang up. I have wasted more time than I care to admit because I was looking for that "teachable moment." Wrong. Never, ever engage this caller. You are not going to change his or her mind through rational thought. I usually say, "Thank you very much for your opinion." Then I hang up. The only example I can give the world is to live my life well. Anyway, being happy really drives your detractors nuts.

- *Complaints:* You thought the reading went well, only to find that your client is refuting the charge on the credit card. You can either call your client to ask what the problem is in an attempt to work it out or you can let it go and not read for the person again. I've done it both ways (when the client canceled payment) and my policy has evolved into a simple one: I never argue because it isn't worth the energy. I do not have to defend my reading skill to anyone. I know my own integrity. Requests for refunds rarely occur. When they do, I always give them.

• *Anger during a reading:* There is a certain distance in a phone reading and it's much easier to misbehave when the conversation isn't face to face. You may have callers who want to hear specific things in the reading or you may tell them something they don't want to hear. Try to remember: nine times out of ten, the anger has nothing whatsoever to do with you. You have just hit someone's "hot button" and you're getting her displaced wrath. Calmly explain that you didn't choose the cards, you are just trying to read them. If your caller isn't ready to hear the information, move on. Don't press it. Keep in mind that you may have planted a seed of knowledge that will help with insight later. If all else fails, tell your client that you are hanging up and issue a refund.

At-Risk Callers

Many people have readings during difficult times in their lives. Some callers may not see many options left. Be careful not to stereotype emotionally unstable callers. Don't expect wailing or an "out of control" personality. The signs of trouble are subtle over the phone and you must listen carefully: nervous speech patterns, long silences, angry comments, confusion or scattered thoughts, needing much reassurance, phrases such as "What's the use?" You may hear crying, but most of the time at-risk callers will converse normally without the dramatics.

You are giving out advice in exchange for money. Perhaps you have an entertainer's license and don't feel obligated or qualified to recognize emergencies. No, you will not be held to as high a degree of legal accountability as a licensed therapist, but as a professional reader, you have the duty of knowing when to stop a reading because professional help is indicated. (More on this in chapter 5.) There are only two psychiatric emergencies in which it is your moral, if not legal, obligation to get outside assistance: the caller is harmful to self, or the caller is harmful to another.[11]

It is not your job to diagnose a psychiatric disorder, but be on alert if your caller mentions any of the following: a previous attempt at suicide, a recent loss or separation, loss of physical health, being widowed or divorced, fired from a job, a history of depression, a clear plan on how to kill herself or harm others (and the plan would be lethal if carried out), a gun in the house, acknowledgment of rage or violent behavior, a history of alcoholism, or fantasies about suicide or homicide. Surprisingly, a person may become calm after the decision to harm herself or others has been made. Pay special attention if your caller talks about killing herself or someone else in a calm manner.[12]

Never ignore a threat to harm one's self or others. It is a myth that people who intend to kill themselves never discuss it. They *do* talk about it! The following guidelines will help you in a time of telephone crisis:

- Take the caller seriously.

- Speak gently and remind the caller that she does have choices. Give her the toll-free number to the suicide prevention hot line and the number to the local psychiatric emergency services (from the list of resources you keep by the phone, of course). Encourage her to call or go to the emergency room for help.

- Take charge of the conversation and remain calm. Breathe deeply.

- Ask if she is taking any medication and if she is combining it with alcohol.

- Directly ask if she intends to harm herself or another. Say that you are concerned about her and, for goodness sake, sound sincere.

- Ask if she has the means to harm herself or another (examples would include access to a gun, drugs, car, rope, knife, poison, etc.).

- Get her phone number and address. Tell her that you are hanging up now because you are calling 911 on her behalf. Then do it! When you place the call, tell the operator exactly what you asked the caller and exactly what the caller said. Don't exaggerate anything. Be factual. Give the dispatcher the name, address, and telephone number of your caller. Let someone trained in crisis intervention make the final decision about taking action.

- If she hangs up on you before you get contact information, call 911 anyway and report exactly what happened. Let trained personnel decide the next move.

- Don't minimize the gravity of the situation in your report: "Oh, he said he was going to off his girlfriend and kill himself, but he didn't sound serious." If he said it, it's serious. You don't want to read about the homicide/suicide in tomorrow's paper.

- Err on the side of caution. Report all threats of harming one's self or harming others; but remember, your only responsibility is to report the suicide or homicide threat to the proper authorities. Let people trained in crisis intervention assess the real danger. Do not, under any circumstances, attempt a face-to-face intervention on your own. You could get killed.

- If it feels right, send healing or protective energy to the caller after you hang up, or say a prayer.

- Despite your best efforts, your caller may carry out the threat of harm. It is not your fault; you cannot control the choices or actions of others. If you called emergency personnel, you have done your part. Let it go, but by all means talk about it to a trusted friend or advisor.

Please note: Paranoid or drug-induced psychoses, and the resultant hallucinogenic voices telling people to harm themselves or others, are entirely different psychiatric conditions. Psychotic episodes require highly skilled intervention. I can't emphasize it enough: don't attempt to diagnose or be a hero. You could get hurt or put someone else in harm's way. Do make that emergency call.

That Old Time-Versus-Money Thing

Without getting into specific technology, there are a few more things to consider when conducting tarot business in cyberspace: How much *money* are you willing to spend on cyberspace tarot? Will you post articles, book or deck reviews, or other promotional materials? Will you offer online classes or sell products from a secure site? It all takes space, and space costs money, so the size of the site and how many pages it has are important considerations. So are cost of site maintenance, access to traffic flow, billing, credit card processing, chargeback protection, bad debt collection, money-back guarantees, issuing refunds, securing the site, adding a shopping cart, and technical support for your site when it crashes (and it will crash).

How much *time* are you willing to spend on cyberspace tarot? Do you have the time to make regular updates, write reviews, and give readings? Will you be able to check your e-mail at least four times per week and respond to your potential clients within forty-eight to seventy-two hours of request? Trust me, if they don't hear from you within a reasonable amount of time, they'll go elsewhere and take their business with them.

Hint: You can use an auto-responder e-mail system. Your visitor receives an automatic e-mail response to any inquiry, something like "Your correspondence is important to me. I'll be communicating with you soon. Thank you for your interest." Consider having two e-mail addresses—one for personal correspondence and one for business—so the lines between work and personal life don't blur. It saves time and avoids confusion. Anyway, your friends will grow weary of auto-response e-mail.

The ways to establish a following on the web are endless, but remember the old adage: If it doesn't cost a lot of money, it will cost a lot of time. Which do you have more of? Honestly answer the question before charging ahead. Pricey cyberspace technologies include chat rooms or message boards. You might offer a tarot essay contest and post the winning essay, but this will be a clock-eater. And please be careful with the offer of free readings. It is often hard to charge money after your service is free. If you do offer free readings, make it for a very limited time and stick to the plan.

A final word to the wise: In the beginning, don't count on your website to be your sole source of income. Think of it as your own business that, just like the Ace of Pentacles, you are building from the ground up. It takes time to build a reputation of excellence, establish trust, and develop a loyal clientele.

Children and the Internet

According to the Federal Trade Commission (FTC), you cannot knowingly respond online to children under the age of thirteen without parental consent.[13] A person must be at least eighteen years of age to buy online from you. (The sticky wicket of reading for minors face-to-face is explored in chapter 5.) To read more about the Children's Online Privacy Protection Act (COPPA), please visit www.ftc.gov/ogc/coppa1.htm

I do not sell online merchandise or readings, but I carry the following disclaimer at the bottom of my home page. Please note that the underlined portions represent links that visitors can click and go directly to the highlighted information:

"The <u>Federal Trade Commission</u> has implemented an online privacy protection act to safeguard children using the Internet. To comply with the <u>Children's Online Privacy Protection Act (COPPA),</u> I cannot knowingly respond to children less than 13 years of age without parental consent. Kids, be honest with me. Deception is bad Karma. Parents, if you don't want your kids to read about new age subjects, adjust your parental control settings. I am not responsible for children who engage in deception, or parents who do not engage in active parenting. To read more about children and Internet safety guidelines, go directly to the <u>KIDZ PRIVACY PAGE</u>."[14]

Ask the Expert

Computer technology changes faster than the weather. I wasn't sure I was qualified to write a techno-chapter. After all, I took a manual typewriter, carbon paper, and lots of Wite-Out to college with me. The information superhighway consisted of a card catalog that took up the first floor of any library. The Net was something a tennis ball flew over. But, as the old saying goes, when in doubt, read the directions. I've taken the liberty of revising it to fit the techno-age: When in doubt, ask the expert!

First, let me introduce you to the expert: Diane Wilkes maintains TarotPassages.com, a comprehensive and informative tarot website. She presents workshops around the country and teaches the tarot in the Philadelphia area. Diane holds a master of arts in English and has been published in numerous magazines. She is the author of the book *Storyteller Tarot*. Artist Arnell Ando beautifully expresses Diane's concept in a majors-only deck of the same name.

Diane is a certified tarot grand master in the American Tarot Association and serves on its editorial board for the ATA's *Tarot Journal*. She's been reading the cards for thirty years and is currently working on her second book titled *Tell Me a Tarot Story: Using the Tarot As a Tool for Creativity*.

I contacted Diane and asked for advice. What should I tell my readers about having a tarot website? She was gracious enough to share her web expertise with me and I pass it along to you with her permission.

CHRISTINE: Thank you for taking the time to share your expertise with me. Establishing a web presence is a daunting task. Please give me your "Top Ten" list of what every tarot reader should know.

DIANE: I'm happy to help in any way I can. I love being a resource. Here goes:

1. Organize or structure your site with growth in mind.

2. Don't assume your visitors have experience using the web. Demarcate links clearly and explain everything.

3. Get your information to search engines, and don't expect your site to skyrocket to the top. You may have to keep after some search engines.

4. Think about your goals for the website before you begin and structure your website to reflect those goals.

5. Don't make your site too busy or fancy. Make it easy to read and attractive. Music and frames can be very annoying. Don't use frames just to use them; consider them a necessary evil, if they're necessary at all.

6. However much time you think you are going to spend on your site, it will probably be more.

7. If you want visitors, you need a hook. Updating on a regular basis increases your chances for repeat, steady visitors. Let your visitors know your update schedule and stick to it. You can also offer polls/games/small prizes to build a visitor base.

8. The web is a big place to bring in visitors; you need to have information they can't find anywhere else on the Internet.

9. If your site is primarily commercial and you're just beginning, you might want to offer free one-card readings for a while to build up a clientele. Draw people to your site by adding content, such as articles, sample readings, book or deck reviews.

10. By all means use the copyright (©) logo on your home page to protect your work, but don't be surprised when you find articles and information that you've offered on your site elsewhere—with someone else's name attached as author. It's a well-known occupational hazard for website owners on the Internet. If there's something you don't want appropriated under any circumstances, don't put it on the web. And a bonus . . .

11. You don't need to learn HTML (hypertext markup language). I use FrontPage by Microsoft, and if you're familiar with Microsoft software, you should be able to learn this program quickly. I understand Dreamweaver is also excellent.

CHRISTINE: Do you also have a Top Ten list for "Please Don't Make the Same Mistakes I Did"?

DIANE: I am fortunate because I inherited Tarot Passages from the wonderful Michele Jackson. I can't take full credit for the quality of the site because she had removed all the kinks before I took over. She also gave workshops on the use of the web and tarot. I learned so much from her.

I would tell newcomers to have some form of computer feedback on how many people visit the site and what pages are visited most frequently. This way, you can adapt your format to suit the visitors' preferences and increase traffic flow. Not that I do that! Book reviews are much less visited than deck reviews, and they take me much longer to write since I have to read the book first. But I continue to write them because I think it's an important service for people who *do* read them.

CHRISTINE: What type of visitor e-mail do you receive?

DIANE: People often e-mail me a question such as, "Is my boyfriend cheating on me?" I write back and give them website addresses for several free computerized online reading sites like Tarot.com, as well as the Free Reading Network, which involves a free reading with a real person. I tell them that I am a professional reader and ask if they would like more information about my rates. I also refer them to my consultation page.

CHRISTINE: What do you do when someone requests a paid reading from you?

DIANE: If someone writes that they want a reading with me in particular, I send the following e-mail:

Dear _____,

Thank you for expressing interest in a tarot reading. We can do the reading in one of three ways: a snail mail reading, an e-mail reading, or, if you have ICQ or Yahoo Instant Messenger, we can do it interactively. This way, you have the opportunity for input and questions in "real time." I accept money orders or money via PayPal.

If you want to see a sample of my reading style, you can go to any of the sample tarot readings I've done on the site. (www.tarotpassages.com/samplereadings.htm) For a half-hour reading, I charge $35.00. For an hour reading, I charge $65.00. If we are doing an interactive reading, that is, through ICQ or Yahoo IM, the reading will probably take longer than if I do it by e-mail.

Ideally, before the reading, you can tell me what you want to focus on during the reading. The more specific you are, the more I can key into your individual needs and issues. Prices vary based on whether the reading is interactive or e-mail. Estimate approximately five minutes per card.

We can create a spread specific to your question(s), or I can do any of the following:

[Types of spreads are listed here.]

If you have a type of deck preference let me know. If the deck you prefer isn't listed, let me know. I may own it. Here are some decks you can choose from:

[Types of decks are listed here.]

If you are getting a snail mail or an e-mail reading, or one via ICQ or Yahoo, I will e-mail you a file with the card images so that you can see the cards as you read what I have written, or as I do the reading. If you have your own tarot deck, or don't want or need to see the card images, or prefer a snail mail color printout of your cards instead of an e-mail attachment, let me know.

You must be 18 years of age or older to order a reading. Your reading is completely confidential. I am enclosing my Code of Ethics, so you have a better understanding of who I am and how I work. I look forward to hearing from you soon.

Take care,
Diane Wilkes
Tarot Passages[15]

CHRISTINE: Readers can find your code of ethics in appendix A and I might add it is wise counsel for all of us. Thanks again for sharing your time, talent, and expertise.

DIANE: My pleasure. I hope it was helpful.

You now have great advice from a lady who's "been there." She included enough information to keep us busy for a very long time. The next chapter covers the legalities of self-employment as you learn "The Business of Tarot."

4 ‖ The Business of Tarot

If at once you have begun, never leave until it's done.
Be it big, or be it small, do it well or not at all.

— Anonymous

In this chapter, we'll cover the legalities of self-employment. You'll explore zoning and licensing laws, keeping legal records, untaxed income, using a computer for business purposes, and the practical and legal considerations of closing your practice. You'll also learn how to work smarter with barter. Let's start by getting organized.

Fibber McGee's Closet

I love to listen to recordings of radio programs from the '30s and '40s in the era before television. Strong visualization skills help me hone my intuitive ability. Old radio programs strengthen my mind's eye because I get to visualize what I hear.

There used to be a show called "Fibber McGee and Molly." Every week poor Molly would plead with Fibber to clean out the closet. Every week old Fibber had some excuse to avoid it. The program ended when Molly opened the dreaded closet door. You never heard such rattling and clatter. You could only imagine what might be falling down on Molly's head, but the ensuing thunder sounded like pots, pans, metal cans, handyman's tools, and probably the kitchen sink. Every week you heard Fibber yell, "Oh, no, Molly, don't open that door!" Every week Molly opened it and got blasted with falling debris. If your office space is the modern-day equivalent of Fibber McGee's closet, it's time to clean house and get organized.

Organizing Your Office Space

Quick, where is your favorite pen and appointment book right now? Can't answer? Please continue reading. I'll never tell you how to organize your tarot card reading space because that's up to you. This is the business chapter, so I'll cover basic needs for an organized workspace. If your office surroundings aren't in order, your business isn't in order. Another way to take the professional out of tarot reader is to appear to others like your life is a train wreck.

Later on, we'll look at itemized tax deductions for tarot readers. For now, know that in order to qualify for a tax deduction on your home office space, the space you set aside for business must be used *only* for that business. Choose a separate room or a specific area for your office space.

A word of warning about declaring portions of rent and utility expenses as itemized tax deductions: If you set up your office at home, talk to an accountant or tax adviser before taking a portion of your homeowner or rent expenses as deductions.[1] The IRS has a tricky formula for figuring out what percentage of expenses you can deduct. After the weather and computer technology, nothing changes faster than tax law.

You needn't spend lots of money setting up your office. Check with the nearest used office furniture store or go to garage sales. Shop around because prices vary. Here are the basics of your physical office (we'll cover the business of computers later):

- A desk or table and comfortable chair

- Telephone and answering machine

- Space for paperwork (shelves, bookcase, or filing cabinet)

- Space for office supplies (Most office supply stores sell inexpensive organizers)

- Appointment book, calendar, and pen

- Typewriter, if you're not using a word processing program (optional)

You'll also need some basic office supplies:

- Telephone book

- Telephone notepad and pencil beside the phone for writing down messages

- Pens and pencils, scissors or letter opener, postage stamps

- #10 business envelopes and paper for business correspondence

- Accounting ledger to keep a record of income and expenses for tax purposes by the week, month, and year (more on this later)

- A book of blank receipts for services rendered and merchandise sold (A receipt is written proof for you, your client, and the IRS)

- One notepad used only for keeping track of where and when you advertised and the response

- Business cards to use for advertising right away

- An attractive flyer or brochure with basic information about your reading services

Keep everything handy and within easy reach. Replenish supplies before you run out. It is most frustrating to reach for the nonexistent stamps at 10 P.M.

The next category I'll call "nice but not necessary" at the start:

- City map if you plan to read in the client's home

- A "tarot-to-go" kit (see chapter 2)

- Calculator for tallying income and expenses or determining reading fees

- Reference books (tarot, psychology, astrology, business, your area of expertise, etc.)

- Letterhead stationery and matching envelopes carrying the name of your business and logo

- At least one locked filing cabinet or box to keep client contact information so you can begin to develop a mailing list for advertising. Because this is confidential information, please be certain the filing box or cabinet is secure. Alphabetize your list.

- I also recommend you devise a system to keep track of how many times your clients request readings. I am hesitant to read for someone more than once a month because this promotes dependency. Every three to six months is better.

Your physical workspace doesn't need to be complicated or expensive, but there are some intangibles to consider: Be honest about what you need to feel good about your enterprise. If a windowless workspace depresses you, don't choose a spot in the far reaches of the basement. What sort of view will help your intuition? How much privacy must you have? What about noise levels? What other things can you provide to make yourself feel as comfortable, creative, and productive as possible? Most importantly, what is the overall effect of the workspace? Is it a spot where you can feel good? A place where you feel like working?

If you are working from home, how will you handle self-discipline and interruptions? Without a time clock or supervisor, it takes inner commitment to go to work every day. The easiest way to "punch in" is to declare business hours and stick to them. It doesn't matter if it's 9 to 5, 9 to 9, 8 P.M. to 10 P.M. or noon to 3. You'll be motivated to work on building a thriving practice if you announce your hours and keep them.

Remember all the stuff I suggested in chapter 2? Keeping office hours will carve out the time to do them and bring you closer to your goals. You can target your markets, prepare a mass mailing, write an ad, design a brochure, prepare a list of community resources, outline your FAQ sheet, or tally your income and expenses—whatever you need to do to keep moving forward. It will also be much easier for potential clients to reach you during set hours.

Building a serious tarot business requires a commitment to the long haul and firm resolve to avoid distractions. Friends and family can equate your being at home with being free to talk. When I'm working, I answer the phone by saying, "Consultations with Christine. How may I help you?" This lets my callers know I mean business. It's up to you to send a clear message. When friends and family see that you are serious, they are less apt to intrude on your work time. Because your tarot business is important to you, put your office hours on your calendar and give them the same priority you give any other pressing engagement. Don't ignore or forget about your work schedule.

If you've grown fond of eating, you *can* find the time to build a thriving tarot practice and still keep your day job. Become a fierce protector of your office hours. When your time for work arrives, use it for work and *not for anything else*. Turn off everything but your business phone or answering machine, lock your door, and block the instant messages. The laundry, dishes, and e-mail can wait. They will still be there when you get back to them. The only real deadline for making your dreams come true is your own death. You are mortal. Start turning your dreams into reality by working toward them today.

Are You a Business?

If you read the cards occasionally for a buck, and do no planning, advertising, or bookkeeping, consider yourself an entertainer. But you've decided you want to be a professional tarot reader. You found out in chapter 1 that you have good reasons for wanting to be self-employed. It's time to put your business together. You can call your tarot reading service a "business" if you'll be supporting your services with a lot of planning, marketing, advertising, coordinating, and accounting. If that describes you, you'll face many decisions and you need a framework in which to make them. That framework is your business.

"Business" is a fuzzy term. As a business owner, you must decide how your business will operate. To see what yours will look like, begin with important basic decisions about your services, which clientele you will serve, and how things will get done. Define your services, deciding what you will and won't do. How broad or how narrow will your range of services be? What is your bottom line? Quality is an important consideration when defining your services. Don't overextend yourself and whatever it is that you do, do it well. There are some tough decisions in defining your services. Remember your reasons for being a professional tarot reader and don't stray from them.

So that there will be no misunderstandings, disputes, or disappointments later, communicate what your services include and exclude. Every business has established policies and your professional tarot reading service should be no different. You have thought about payment and refund policies, but there are other issues to decide as well.

Some decisions can be made in advance, while others will surface and surprise you as time goes by. Put your policies and procedures in writing. When a client asks you why you don't make house calls at midnight, you can honestly say it is a business policy to conclude all in-home readings by 9 P.M. (or whatever time you choose) due to safety concerns.

To get you started, here are a few things to consider when writing your policy and procedures. They are based on my own experiences and I am sure you'll think of others.

• Payment policy

• Bounced check policy with stipulated fee for recovery

- Refund policy

- Reading hours, including days of the week

- Office hours

- Cancellation policy, both yours and your client's

- Safety procedures for in-home readings

- Initial client interviews: How long are you willing to spend answering questions? Will you charge after a certain amount of time or are they free?

- Emergency plans and payment policies: Whom will you call when you're sick and can't get out of bed to do a reading? How will your backup be paid?

- Last-minute appointments: Will you accept them if it means interfering with your personal or family time? If so, will you charge more?

- Children, yours and theirs: Does a screaming two-year-old destroy your concentration? What will you do if your client's child breaks something while you read in your home or office? What will you do if your child does the same in someone else's home?

- Will you carry personal liability insurance? What happens when someone slips on the ice in front of your home? What if you are injured on a client's property? Who pays the medical bills in both these instances? What happens when someone sues you for being a quack?

- Will you allow the client's "guests" to sit in on a reading? What will you do when the information turns painfully private?

- Holiday surcharges: Will you charge extra for readings done on major holidays? Are you willing to read on holidays?

This isn't a complete list of policies and procedures because there isn't one way to run a tarot business. And don't forget, policies can always be changed. What works in the beginning may need revision later as you learn, gain experience, and grow.

Are You Legal?

The most common legal structures for small businesses include sole proprietorships, partnerships, corporations, and limited liability companies.[2] What legal structure will your tarot consultation service take and why is it important? Because it defines ownership, and when more than one person is involved in a business, it also determines relationships, authority, control, responsibility, and distribution of profits or losses. Tax consequences and liabilities also vary with each of these legal structures.

As a general rule, operate as a sole proprietorship if you are working alone, or if you'll include other readers in your tarot business but wish to retain authority to make important decisions. If you're concerned about responsibility for your coworker's bad decisions, incorporate to limit liability, keeping in mind that a corporation must be chartered to do business by the state. When deciding on a partnership, ask yourself the following questions: Can you maintain a relationship with your partner when you're sharing responsibility, control, profits, and losses? Will you trust another's commitment, contributions, and judgment? Are you willing to be responsible for your partner's actions and debts? Please refer to appendix C to learn more about business, including its legal structures.

Let's look closer at sole proprietorship because it is the most common legal structure used by small businesses and the easiest to set up. As sole proprietor, you own the business. In fact, you *are* the business, whether you work alone or not. You have total control and authority. You are completely responsible for what happens and you can't avoid liability. All profits and losses from the business pass over to your personal income tax returns because the business doesn't file a return or pay taxes. If you have no employees, you do not need to apply for a federal ID number. In fact, if you do nothing whatsoever to formalize another legal business structure and you work alone, you become a sole proprietorship.

The advantage of a sole proprietorship is obvious: bureaucracy is minimal because you need not file with government agencies, although some states may require you to register and apply for a business license (refer to next section). The main disadvantage of a sole proprietorship is the unlimited liability in the event of a lawsuit or financial loss. As a tarot reader, ask yourself what type of losses your reading service might cause in light of your personal assets. What do you risk losing?

It is entirely possible to determine your business structure by yourself and save legal fees, just as you do the research and leg work for registering your business name. It is best, however, to consult at least once with a lawyer, tax specialist, or accountant before deciding which structure is best for you. There is usually only a small charge for a one-time consultation and the discussion will help you make an informed decision about your business.

Lions and Tigers and Bears, Oh My

Just as Dorothy and the gang discovered, hidden obstacles lurk on the journey to Oz. At this point, you've outlined the services you'll provide and selected the legal structure your business will take. You've met all the requirements for beginning your tarot business, right? Not quite. Depending on where you'll provide service and where your office is located, there are still a few more things to do. As you read this section, remember that I am not writing about someone who casually reads the cards for a few friends. I am directing the information to those of you who want to be in business for yourself as full-time professional tarot consultants.

Every state is different when it comes to licensing requirements, permits, zoning laws, and prohibitive rules affecting your practice.[3] In fact, licensing and zoning laws vary at the local level of city and county government within a state. In Key West, Florida, for example, a tarot reader must purchase an entertainer's license. In southwestern Ohio, no license is required, but most readers advertise "For entertainment purposes only" to cover any potential liability. In still other states, you can charge money for a reading only if the readings are part of a religious practice. You can get around many licensing laws this way, but I do not recommend it unless you are truly reading the cards as part of your religion. Honesty is always the best policy.

The surest way to know if you're meeting local, county, and state requirements is to contact all cities and smaller communities having city halls, and counties where you will be providing service (found in either the blue or government pages of your phone book; some states offer a one-stop business permit center). Ask if any licenses or permits are required. Be prepared to explain your tarot reading service in a concise and professional way. When contacting the city in which you live, ask if a home occupation permit is required if you intend to do most of the readings at your place of residence. Better yet, call your Chamber of Commerce and obtain a checklist for starting a small business in your area.

Remember in chapter 1 when we looked at combining tarot and another service such as aromatherapy? A vendor's license may be required of all businesses making retail sales of tangible property.[4] In other words, if you sell those aromatherapy oils or herbs to your clients, you need a permit to do so. In most states for a small fee, a temporary license is available for short-term trade shows, festivals, and fairs conducted away from your home county. If you only read the cards, you do not need a vendor's license because you are not selling a tangible product.

Now to zoning laws and building permits. I can't emphasize this enough: Contact your township or municipality zoning inspector to learn about zoning restrictions *before* you start your tarot business in your home, open up your service in an office, or remodel your current space. Building permits certify the safe operation of your business and ensure the safety of your customers. To illustrate, is the entrance to your building wheelchair accessible? Zoning ordinances divide a geographical area into sections where various businesses or activities are allowed or prohibited.[5] For example, a noisy industrial plant can't set up shop automatically in a quiet residential neighborhood. Zoning laws also prevent "nuisances" from doing business in residential communities and your community may define tarot card reading as a nuisance!

Every locale has different zoning and building laws and it isn't always clear who issues the various permits. Some areas are strict while others are not. Zoning laws may not even become important until someone in your locale complains to city hall that you are reading the devil's picture cards or your customers are parking on private lawns.

To make it even more confusing, ordinances are amended frequently. Just because another tarot reader or astrologer has an office in your area, it doesn't mean you have permission to do the same. The astrologer could have been in business before a change was made in the zoning ordinance and she was permitted to stay. You, however, may be unwelcome.

Home offices are even trickier. If you expect to read in your home, you may face restrictions regarding: the amount of traffic your business generates, street parking, signs in front of your house, the number of clients allowed in your home at any one time, hours of operation, and whether or not you have a separate office entrance with an attached bathroom.[6] Check your deed or rental agreement. Never adopt a "wait and see" attitude about zoning; you could find yourself in a lot of legal hot water, not to mention loss of all that money you spent remodeling.

So how can you tell which ordinances pertain to your tarot reading practice? Call the Chamber of Commerce in your area and ask for a list of the types of permits you need to start the kind of service(s) you plan, or at least learn the names of appropriate contacts. Go to the library and research. Whatever you do, be clear on zoning, licensing, and building permits or you could end up in front of the city council like the lady from Moraine. Read on . . .

The Lady from Moraine

Amanda Hamilton didn't know the consequence of opening her meta-physical shop in the small town of Moraine, Ohio. Her shop of twelve years had burned down in Dayton, and she relocated to the nearby rural community. Hamilton applied for a business permit, opened Everything Under the Moon, and began offering $20 tarot readings.

Shortly after, the Moraine city council began drafting a city ordinance to enact an old law that banned anyone from charging a fee to predict the future or hold séances, and required anyone practicing without charging a fee to first register with the chief of police. "Charging a fee to predict the future" included the practices of palm and tarot card reading, runes, astrological chart interpretation, and horoscopes. "Holding séances" included any attempt to communicate with departed spirits in any manner.[7]

Hamilton notified Raymond Vasvari, legal director for the American Civil Liberties Union in Ohio. Vasvari appeared before the city council to point out that the ordinance raised some serious First Amendment questions because it sought to prohibit artistic expression and freedom of speech and religion, and imposed itself onto people's spiritual beliefs. Hamilton told the council that, with the wording of the ordinance, anyone who owned tarot cards would have to register with the chief of police before reading the cards for friends at the kitchen table. She added that certain groups in the area, such as Native Americans or Wiccans, would be subject to arrest for trying to communicate with their dead ancestors or in assisting others to do the same.[8]

Hundreds of pagans, including members of the Witches Against Religious Discrimination, crowded the Moraine government center to address the ordinance. Regular attendees of the Moraine city council meetings became angry because of the number of pagans who were allowed to speak and explain their practices. The regulars seemed especially troubled by references comparing the right to pagan observances with the right to practice Christianity. Arthur Powers, a former councilman, walked out of the meeting muttering, "We don't have to listen to this garbage."[9]

This little tale has a happy ending. After listening to all sides speak, the Moraine city council set aside the ordinance to ban fortune telling or "predicting for a fee."[10] I tell you the story because the ordinance would have enacted an old law *that was already on the books*. Ms. Hamilton may have had no trouble in Dayton, Ohio, but she moved to another city with another set of rules. She did not know of the prohibitive law until she applied for a business permit and opened her doors.

Yes, good finally came out of this mess and the First Amendment remains intact, but what would have happened if the ordinance had passed? Would she have been forced to close or change her business? Enlisting the aid of the American Civil Liberties Union to repeal the old law *before* she opened her shop could have saved her a lot of time and lost revenue. When setting up your own practice, please remember the lady from Moraine.

The Other Sure Thing

As the old saying goes, there are only two certainties in life: death and . . . Please stay on top of your taxes. You are working with untaxed income and it is easy to spend money without allowing for taxes. Many readers pay quarterly taxes to avoid large payments at the end of the year. When it comes to income tax, you can run, but you cannot hide.

You'll be covered if you open a separate savings account and deposit between 20 to 30 percent of your income each month. The required payment probably won't be 30 percent, but it's better to be safe than sorry. You'll have a nice bonus or refund at the end of the year. And don't forget to allow for city, county, and state taxes too.

The best advice I can offer is to speak with an accountant or tax adviser. Educate yourself and pay your taxes. (Grumbling is allowed.) It is unwise to try to hide income or spend money that belongs to Uncle Sam. Tax evasion carries serious criminal consequences, including imprisonment. It isn't worth the risk.

The Internal Revenue Service has a huge website with a keyword search capacity. The FAQ (frequently asked questions) section has content specific to small business owners, including business deductions. Type in "www.irs.gov" and click on "FAQs" from the home page. Once at the FAQ page, click on "Individuals" or "Businesses," depending on how you have set up your legal structure. If you are the sole proprietor, you are the business, and your deductions will be on your individual tax return. To itemize, you must use Form 1040. To make estimated quarterly payments, use Form 1040ES.

I have taken generic tax laws that apply to all small businesses and reworded them to fit the business of professional tarot readers. (I also got this approved by my certified public accountant.) The information is based on how I organize my own taxes, both as a writer and as a professional tarot reader. The following U.S. small business guideline is general and current at press time, but tax laws are always in flux. Last year's deduction is this year's violation. Check this year's tax law before itemizing or deducting anything. And, of course, if you are reading this as a citizen of another country, the tax laws of your government apply.

In the United States, tax deductions for small businesses may only be taken if you establish yourself as a business. A tarot reader who earns little at reading the cards will have to prove that she is a professional and not indulging in a hobby. Uncle Sam doesn't allow us to deduct the expense of our hobbies. Darn, I was contemplating getting a grand piano . . .

If the Internal Revenue Service believes your tarot reading is a hobby or pastime, your deductions are limited to the amount of your hobby income. It works like this: Let's say you make $500 reading the cards this year, but you spend $1500 on a new computer. You can take a $1500 deduction for the computer, right? Wrong. You can take only a $500 deduction because that's the amount of income your hobby produced.

The tax law does offer ways to prove your tarot reading service is a business, not a hobby. If you've made a profit from reading the cards in any three years out of the last five, you win. Even if you can't pass the three-out-of-five-year test, you can convince Uncle Sam that tarot reading is a business and not a hobby *if*[11]

- you run your little business like a business, with financial records, letterhead, business cards, and other evidence that you're serious;

- you don't have a string of high-expense, low-income years stretching back unbroken in history;

- your claimed expenses don't include the frivolous, the outrageous, or the mostly pleasurable (sorry, no lunch deductions to discuss your tarot business with a friend . . . unless your friend is also your certified public accountant or lawyer or someone directly related to the operation and betterment of your tarot business);

- you're good enough at reading the cards and spend enough time reading the cards to be taken seriously as a person intent on making a living as a tarot reader.

To complicate the matter, if you are an employee of someone else's business, you cannot make itemized business deductions. For example, if you read the cards full-time as an employee of a New Age bookstore, you cannot make itemized business deductions. Can you still read at the store? Sure, but you must be in business for yourself to claim itemized deductions. In this case, the bookstore is simply the place you have chosen to be self-employed. That said, the following are considered legitimate itemized tax deductions for small business owners if you keep meticulous records of the expenditures and use Form 1040 or 1040ES:[12]

- Office rent and its heating bill and utilities, if you rent space for the express purpose of reading the cards or running your business

- Office and computer supplies

- Computer or office equipment

- Telephone expenses related to tarot reading

- Books, magazines, and reference materials for your reading service

- Photocopying related to running your business

- Memberships in professional tarot organizations

- Postage related to tarot reading, such as the mass mailing of your flier to advertise

- Business meals (Don't overuse; the IRS looks closely at this one.)

- Reimbursable mileage expense. If you read the cards outside of your home, you can be reimbursed for those miles. To calculate the reimbursable mileage expense, record the number of miles to your client and back home again and multiply that number by the current IRS-allowed rate. At press time it was 27 cents per mile. For this to be a legitimate claim, you must keep accurate mileage records, including dates and places. (I don't bother because it is too much work.)

- Tax preparation (Yes, if someone else prepares your taxes, their fee is a deduction.)

- Travel related to your professional reading service. This includes anything that makes you a better reader or businessperson, such as travel to tarot conferences, workshops, or business seminars. It also includes airfare, meals, hotels, car rental expenses, and mileage when you travel to read the cards, as noted earlier.

- Educational expenses. This covers the price of any small business or counseling courses or workshops, any reference books you buy to improve your skills, or any related educational fee that makes you a better reader or businessperson.

A final word about taxes: E-file, the electronic filing of income taxes, is common now, as are tax software programs such as TurboTax.

You can read more about electronic filing at the IRS website. If you decide to use a tax software program, you will need to upgrade the software package every year because of tax law and tax table changes.

Bookkeeping 101

You've seen by now that there is a lot more to being a professional tarot consultant than reading the cards. In fact, your tarot reading service is the tip of the iceberg. Your tarot *business* lies beneath it—all the planning, organizing, and accounting that support the service.

Remember all the reasons you are starting a business from chapter 1: love of the cards, profit, the sincere desire to help people, and the thrill of being in business for yourself, and so on. In other words, you want to make money while enjoying yourself. "Making money" is a dangerous phrase because too many readers equate it with collecting reading fees. In this book, "making money" is about realizing a profit.

By now you know that there is a big difference between collecting fees (generating revenue) and true profit, and that difference is costs or expenditures. For example, it is great that you made $200 reading the cards today, but if your $500 office rent is due tomorrow, you did not "make money." The only way to make money, that is, to make a profit, is to control both revenue (how much money you generate) and costs (your expenditures). So how do you keep track of revenue and costs? By keeping accurate records, she grumbles.

The good news is that keeping accurate business records does not have to be complicated. The law doesn't require any special kinds of records and you can choose any system that clearly shows your income. There is no "best" way to keep records except that your method is accurate and consistent. Use any bookkeeping plan that makes sense to you—the simpler, the better.

If you like working with computers, you may want to buy accounting software, such as Peachtree Complete Accounting, and let technology do all the work for you. For managing personal finances and keeping track of spending, try a personal finance program like Quicken. Be aware that opinions vary greatly on the worth of accounting and financial software programs. I read reviews of QuickBook Pro at Amazon.com and it ranked from one star (don't bother) to five stars (the best). Ask around before you buy.

Expensive software isn't necessary, especially when you're first starting out. Regardless of your chosen method, your bookkeeping system should include a summary of your business transactions including gross income, credits, and deductions. This summary can be made in something as simple as accounting journals, ledgers, or checkbooks.

Invoices and receipts document purchases, sales, payroll, and any other business transactions. Invoices and receipts contain the information you need to record in your books. (You can buy inexpensive, ready-made invoices and receipts at any office supply store.) It is important to keep copies of invoices and receipts because they support the entries you make both in your books and on your tax return. The key to keeping it simple is to record your bookkeeping information in a timely and orderly fashion, such as every day or every week, and add up the totals at the end of every month.

Don't throw away any of your receipts because they verify all your bookkeeping entries and come in handy during the rare client dispute. They will also be needed for tax audits. In fact, the IRS recommends that you keep all records for at least five years. (Some references recommend seven.) I work it like this: Let's say it is April 2002. My yearly filing for 2001 is done in April 2002, so I throw away my records for 1995 (2001 minus six years) in April 2002. I am left with five years' worth of records.

I don't know about you, but little bits of crumpled paper lying everywhere drive me crazy, so I organize. I buy two large expandable envelope-type portfolios and label one income and the other expenses. I mark each pocket by the month. Then, when I've recorded my amounts in the ledger (see below), I throw the receipts in their respective pockets. This saves a ton of confusion later when I'm trying to figure out what I spent or what I earned. If I don't save the receipts I have no way of verifying my entries in the ledger. For more information, please visit the official IRS website.

The following are types of records you should keep; the term "supporting documents" refers to invoices and receipts, including your checkbook:[13]

- *Gross receipts*: The income you have received from your business. Keep any supporting documents that show the amounts and sources of your gross receipts.

- *Purchases*: Items you buy and resell to customers. Examples include aromatherapy oils, books, or any other merchandise that you purchase and resell to your clients. Supporting documents need to show that the amount you paid was for purchases.

- *Expenses*: The cost you incur (other than purchases) to carry on your business. Supporting documents show the amount paid and that the amount was for business expenses.

- *Assets*: The property, such as office equipment or furniture, which you own and use in your business. You need records to verify ownership; you'll use these records to compute the annual depreciation on them. Documents support the gain or loss if and when you sell the assets. For example, the value of your computer depreciates every year. If you sell your computer and buy a new one, you need to keep records of all transactions, including what you did with your old computer. If you gave the old one to charity, it can be a tax deduction. I suggest you consult with a tax expert for advice on figuring the depreciation of your assets because it does make a difference on your tax return.

Okay, now you know some of the records you should keep, but what exactly are "simple" bookkeeping procedures? The IRS suggests the following steps to create an uncomplicated record-keeping system for your business[14] (Yeah, I know. Who can believe that the words "uncomplicated" and "IRS" are used in the same sentence?):

- Use prenumbered sales invoices to track sales to customers (in this case, to track the purchase of your tarot readings and other services). Keep a copy of each invoice that you give a client for your own records. Total your income every week, month, and year and keep a record of the totals. While we're on the subject of receipts, be sure to write down the date of the receipt, the client's name and address, the form of payment, the length of the reading, and the total payment. Give the top copy to your client.

- Deposit *in full* all your customer payments in the bank, whether received by cash or check. By doing this, you can determine your income at the end of the month or year by adding up all your deposits and matching them to the sales invoice totals. (I bought an inexpensive "For Deposit Only" rubber stamp at the office supply store. I endorse each check and use the stamp underneath my signature.)

- Maintain a bank account that is separate from your personal account and use it for only your business expenses. Balance your bank statements every month for both deposits made and checks written. Keep your monthly bank statements. This lets the bank do some of the record keeping for you.

- Pay for all business expenses using checks from your business bank account.

- Use your business-account check register as a basic cash payments register.

- Consider investing in a multicolumn ledger book to keep track of expenses. When creating column titles, choose ones that you will use a lot, like office supplies, advertising, and rent, if you rent office space for your readings. Label the last column "Miscellaneous" for any payments that don't fit the other columns and explain what they are.

By using this basic system throughout the year for income and expenses, you can simply add up the columns and get the correct amounts for your gross receipts and business expenses to use for your tax return. This system also helps you compute your quarterly estimated taxes.

Whether keeping track by computer or pen and paper, preparation for income tax time is as much fun as having a root canal. But with a little bit of organization and simple bookkeeping, we can all be ready for the other certainty in life. For more information, refer to IRS Publication 583, "Starting a Business and Keeping Records." It can be downloaded as a PDF file at www.irs.gov.

The Business of Computers

I am a freelance technical writer, university writing instructor, and professional tarot consultant. All my income is untaxed. I chose a paper-and-pencil bookkeeping system that made sense to me. The office procedures described in this chapter have served me well, but that doesn't mean they are the only game in town. Computers and high-quality printers save time and labor in operating your own business. With the advent of laptops and palm pilots, you also have the advantage of being portable. Home PCs can be used in a wide variety of ways to enhance your success as a professional tarot reader. Here are just a few suggestions. With a personal computer and an Internet connection, you can[15]

- track the results of your advertising methods;
- build a customer database;
- manage and easily revise your address book;
- maintain mailing lists (both snail mail and e-mail);
- print your appointment schedules and address labels;
- keep accurate financial records;

- design and print your own invoices and receipts;

- create your own business cards, fliers, newsletters, and other special documents with desktop publishing software such as Broderbund's Print Shop and Press Writer;

- access information and conduct online research;

- communicate with other tarot professionals;

- visit tarot websites and chat rooms;

- advertise your services online;

- conduct web tarot readings;

- stay abreast of new publications, books, decks, and theory;

- locate and register for pertinent seminars, workshops, conferences, and classes;

- join a professional tarot organization by signing up online;

- purchase continuing education materials and books;

- and much, much more as the technology continues to evolve.

There are a few drawbacks to having a computer, including the purchase price.

Software isn't cheap, either. I have heard that "to err is human, but to really foul things up takes a computer." Computers are machines and they break down, usually at the most inopportune times. Upkeep can be very expensive.[16] If you're a baby boomer like me, you weren't taught how to use a computer in school. It will take a lot of your time to learn how to work with one. Another consideration is the loss of privacy. I believe in the charm of distance and I don't always appreciate e-mail invasions.

For me, the biggest computer negatives are obsolescence and the pressure and expense to upgrade both hardware and software. My brother-in-law gave me my first computer. It was a pre-Internet 1988

MS-DOS and it had no modem or mouse. Everything was done with keyboard commands. I used it for the word processing program. I bought my first computer at the end of 1997 and started with Windows 95, a Pentium II processor, and AOL Version 3.0. In less than three months, Windows 98 appeared, along with Pentium IIX and AOL Version 4.0. My expensive purchases were already outdated.

A computer is not an essential piece of equipment for a professional tarot reading service. This is especially true if you're in the beginning stages of planning. You'll want to keep start-up expenses to a minimum. But because computers are so widespread today, the chances are good that you already own one. If so, by all means, use it in your business. Managed growth will be much easier when you have computer options available. If you don't currently have a computer, I suggest that you wait to buy one until you are established and committed to growing your tarot business.

Barter Is Smarter

Barter is the exchange of goods or services and is a cashless transaction.[17] Trading service for service can be gratifying, but only if you want what you get in the trade. To avoid resentment, be certain both of you believe the trade is worthwhile and equitable. The best trade is when both people think they're getting the better end of the deal. It might be for a meal, a service, an exchange of readings, or a material object.

Barter affords you a legal method to conserve your cash and is a good way to expand your client base. People who might never consider a tarot reading might do so if no money is exchanged, and those clients can refer you to cash-paying customers. You can trade for office supplies, flower deliveries, business cards, haircuts, brochure design, printing ads, massage, tax preparation, office furniture, housecleaning, or a workshop.

When bartering, it is a good idea to exchange vouchers for two reasons: You must claim barters on your tax returns (and therefore need a record) and you have a written agreement for a delayed exchange.

For example, let's say you have traded a reading for the mass printing of your flyer. You don't have the flyer ready yet, but you give the reading. When you have the flyer prepared, you can redeem the voucher in a simple transaction. Most people have good hearts, but a written record of your trade prevents selective amnesia at collection time.

Treat barter as cash because it's taxable income. The trade dollars you spend on business expenses are deductible. Don't pay more for an item through barter than you would with cash. In other words, don't give a $50 reading for a $10 box of stationery. And, above all, don't accept bartering transactions you can't or don't want to fulfill. For instance, an ad agency wants you to provide ongoing readings for its employees for a year in exchange for a beautiful, professional brochure design. It may be tempting at first, but don't do it. Seven months from now, when the brochure no longer has the correct phone number but you still have five months to go on the trade, you will regret the decision.

In trade transactions, it's true you don't always get what you want when you want it. But with a little creativity, patience, and flexibility, you can barter your way to having a lot of the services you need to run a small business.

Closing Your Business

With planning and effort, you can have a long and rewarding career as a professional tarot reader. But times change and we change with them. Family needs, burnout, job opportunities, or illness are but a few reasons to stop. I suggest that instead of "just quitting," you take the time to formally close your business. Don't disappear off the map. When clients find out you no longer read because your number is disconnected, you serve to perpetuate the stereotype of the fly-by-night fortune-teller.

It may be hard to sell your tarot business. In retail, you have a store with a lease or mortgage, an inventory, merchandise and equipment, besides your business name and reputation. In a service like tarot reading, the assets are more intangible: You may have a logo and name, established policies, a client list, and your reputation. If you have worked out of your home, you most likely have only a client list to sell.

Announce to the tarot community that you are closing your business. Call or send a professional note to other readers letting them know you have a client list for sale. Be selective because your good name is attached to the list. You can price the list in one of two ways: either sell it outright for a flat fee based on a set amount per name, or determine the amount of revenue you received from each client over the last year, average it, and sell the list based on a percentage of income per name.[18]

In the second method, the buyer makes a down payment and makes the final payment at the end of a specified time. Get this in writing with two signatures, yours and the buyer's. Although a flat fee of so much per name results in a faster payment and easier sale, the percentage method eventually results in a higher price for the seller.

Discuss which option of selling is right for you with an accountant or attorney.

Whether you sell your client list or not is up to you. Regardless of your choice, close your tarot reading service with style and grace. Remember your reasons for wanting to be a professional reader. You wanted to be a credit to the industry and elevate the art of reading the cards to a professional status. Let the same commitment to excellence guide you as you leave the business:

- Notify your clients of your decision to close your business. Suggest other readers.

- If you are selling your client list, inform your customers in writing and ask if they want their names excluded from the list. Respect all decisions and carry out their wishes. Recommend the new reader and thank them for their business.

- Place an ad announcing the closing of your business. If you have sold your client list, recommend that reader in your announcement.

- Notify any professional organizations or businesses that you are closing your business (the organizations or businesses that might refer clients to you). A good way to determine who might refer someone to you is to backtrack your advertising campaign. Where did you place an ad or leave a brochure, business card, or flyer? It is both annoying and embarrassing for an organization or business, such as a New Age bookstore, the Jungian Society, or herbal shop, to give out incorrect information.

Closing your tarot reading service can pack an emotional wallop. Your intellect may know it is the right thing to do, but your heart can tell you otherwise. You have put so much of yourself into building a tarot practice. Letting it go may feel like part of you has died. Keep in mind that you will never know how many people you have helped or how you have touched and changed lives. The decisions you make and actions you take each and every day will affect the outcome of your business. You can take pride in knowing that you have done your very best, that you left your clients, and the world of tarot, better than when you found them.

In this chapter you have learned how to run and close a professional tarot reading service. In the next chapter, you'll explore the counseling aspect of reading the cards, including the special considerations of counseling clients in crisis. We'll begin by examining the unspoken contract between two people.

5 ‖ Counseling Clients

Learn your theories as well as you can, but put them
aside when you touch the miracle of the living soul.

— Carl Jung

This chapter explores reading for another in detail. Knowledge of psychology and counseling techniques is needed to handle emotionally charged issues with intelligence.

A professional reader is able to distinguish between a "normal" crisis (stressful but predictable parts of life) and a true emergency, such as the threat of suicide. The focus of this chapter is on recognizing a true crisis, maintaining a state of calm, knowing what to do, and keeping a list of healthcare resources close by, including emergency numbers. If you do short readings in quick succession all day long, you'll find a helpful section called "The Ten-Minute Reader." This chapter concludes with a look at special considerations when reading for minors.

No other section of this book gave me more writing fits than this chapter. I rewrote it at least a half-dozen times. I don't pretend to be a Ph.D. psychologist. I am not board certified in psychiatry. Yes, I have a four-year bachelor's degree in psychology, but that hardly qualifies me to hang out my shingle as a therapist. Yes, I have experience counseling others, both as a registered nurse and as a professional tarot reader, but that doesn't give me the final word on anything. Please keep my short-comings in mind as you read *one woman's opinion* on how to counsel clients. Decide what makes sense to you and discard the rest.

The Unspoken Contract

All our relationships with others can be viewed in terms of contracts, and the relationships you have with your clients are no exception. The relationship contract is made up of unstated, usually unconscious, agreements between people about how they will act with each other, including what they will and won't say and do.[1]

Healthy, positive relationships have clearly established contracts of honesty and support between two people. There is room for self-expression without fear of judgment or reprisal, as well as healthy concern for the other. On the other hand, codependent relationships are created through negative contracts that limit, trap, use, control, or intimidate the people in them. They block creativity, personal expression and freedom, and interfere with the natural growth of each person involved.

We all have positive and negative contracts in our lives. The areas of our lives that flow smoothly and fulfill us are the areas where we have positive contracts with others. The areas where we have problems are the areas where we have created negative contracts with others based on our attitudes and negative worldview. The primary reason for neg-ative contracts is to avoid certain feelings we do not want to have.

A contract, once set up, is placed in motion and remains in motion. Each time a negative contract is fulfilled, it serves to validate a nega-tive frame of reference. The negative belief grows stronger each time we circle through another negative experience. Let's say a child whose mother severely punishes her grows up to believe that all women are cruel. Her early life experience of the primary woman in her life, her mother, taught her that. As an adult, she may set up negative contracts that keep women at a distance, or she will get into relationships with cruel women. She may even become cruel to other women herself. All these relationships will prove her belief that women are cruel.

Try this test: Think of the people in your life. Which ones require you to play a certain role or act a certain way? This is the first sign of a negative contract. Now think of the people with whom you can completely be yourself. You don't have to hide anything or convince them of anything, yet you know that they will honestly tell you whatever they think of a given situation, even if you don't like it. This is a sign of a positive contract. Your ideal goal as a professional tarot reader is to establish the qualities of a positive contract—honesty, support, trust, freedom of expression—with each of your clients.

Tarot is a mirror to your soul and a reflection of you. Think of the tarot as a mirror extension of yourself, because your life is a reflection of your beliefs. Interpretation of the tarot symbols is in the eye of the beholder. Your own life experiences will shape your interpretations of the cards. Is the Tower (#16) in tarot the tower of destruction or the stroke of liberation? Is the Sun (#19) representative of the light needed for nourishment and life, or does it mean the scorching heat that lays waste to a desert? Does the Three of Cups mean celebration or alcoholism? It will depend on your frame of reference.

The unintentional projection of our personal pain, or negative contract, can occur while reading tarot for others. Use caution when reading the cards for another. Be aware of your own issues and prejudices. Don't fall into the trap of "inflicting" a tarot reading onto others. As you address your own wounds, remember that the most powerful technique you can use to help people is to determine what issues they reflect in you and heal those issues in yourself.[2]

Self-awareness is a lifelong process. Just because we emerge wiser from one crisis doesn't mean we have completed our soul-work. As long as we live, we will continue to have unexpected challenges and opportunities to develop wisdom. It is through our *ongoing* conscious awareness of personal pain—and courageous acts of self-healing—that we learn compassion, forgiveness, and love. Then we are able to emerge with the qualities of a healer, counselor, and professional tarot reader. Powerful reading does not originate with a pack of cards. Rather, it is the use of self in a loving and compassionate way that provides us with our most powerful instrument for reading the cards, counseling, and helping others.

Learning from Lucy

Charles Schulz, creator of the *Peanuts* comic strip, was a wise man, and Lucy was one of my favorite characters. She dispensed wisdom as she stood behind a sign that read "Psychiatric Help—5 Cents." But mostly, she just showed up and paid attention. As tarot readers, we have a lot to learn from Lucy.

In her wonderful book *The Tarot: Methods, Mastery and More*, Cynthia Giles bases the qualities of a successful tarot reader on Angeles Arriens' *Four-Fold Way:*[3]

- Show up

- Pay attention

- Tell the truth

- Be open to outcomes

Showing up means choosing to be present with the cards, the client, and the unfolding event. It is the Way of the Warrior who is leader, protector, and explorer. We pay attention to what the cards are presenting, not what we personally think. It is the Way of the Healer who gives heart and meaning through the power of love.

We tell the truth when we speak honestly without shame or judgment, rather than trying to control or make a point. It is the Way of the Visionary who creates and communicates. And finally, we remain unattached and open to outcomes, without taking a position, to allow our seeker personal responsibility and freedom of choice. It is the Way of the Teacher who has wisdom and detachment.

Try this: Select a tarot card to represent each of the qualities of a successful reader. For example, which cards represent Warrior, Healer, Visionary, and Teacher to you? It's not a trick question and there are no wrong answers. The cards you choose will be based on your own tarot philosophy and frame of reference. Once you've made your selection, meditate with them one at a time and make an entry in your journal about each. How would each of them conduct a tarot consultation? You'll learn much about the qualities you bring to the reading table.

Handle with Care

Knowing the meaning of the tarot cards, how they relate to one another in a layout, and the ability to weave a narrative are prerequisites for becoming a professional reader. But knowledge of the cards alone is not enough to be a pro. Whether you are reading free for friends or charging money, you are using your understanding of the tarot as a counseling tool because you are influencing other people's lives with your knowledge. Professional tarot readers have a moral and ethical responsibility to develop awareness of the counseling process and build counseling skills.

If you are planning on using the tarot directly with other people, you are exposing yourself to situations where people in need will turn to you for help. Without extensive psychological training, you will have to deal with troubled individuals—the confused, the immature, the suffering, the grieving—who so often look to tarotists, astrologers, and psychics for guidance. Even if you define yourself as a reader, and not a counselor, you will still have significant influence upon your clients' conceptions of life.

Knowledge of psychology and counseling techniques are needed to handle emotionally charged issues with intelligence. This knowledge allows you to phrase a reading so that the client can relate to the information and feel empowered to change what is no longer useful, or build upon existing strengths. It is wise to enroll in one or more counseling courses, attend workshops, and read books on the counseling process. Please refer to appendix C for suggestions.

Most people who practice divination with the tarot for any length of time find that it takes on the character of therapy.[4] The healing emphasis of divination is on the emotional, psychological, and spiritual life. People work through problems, explore thoughts, feelings, and intuitions, and formulate strategies much like they would in a therapist's office. During a professional tarot reading set in a healing atmosphere, time is precious and the space is special because it is protected from the outside world.

On the surface, people have tarot readings for fun, on a whim, out of curiosity, to be entertained, to catch a glimpse of the future, or just to talk about life. On a deeper level, people have tarot readings because they want a private place to talk about problems, reveal secrets, or discuss concerns. They may express feelings and thoughts that they do not want to share with others. The client may feel more comfortable giving this information to a stranger rather than a friend or therapist. As a professional tarot reader, you respect privacy and confidentiality and you give the client a safe place to think, feel, and make decisions without violating the sacred trust the client has placed with you.

Your role, as professional reader, is to interpret the client's cards and feed this symbolic knowledge back to the client for her consideration. Your reading will make it possible for the client to confront and examine difficult or upsetting realities about herself and work through difficulties in a more independent manner. This puts the power to change—through awareness, growth, and action—squarely back where it belongs: in the hands of the client.

By emphasizing the subjective meaning of a card (thoughts and feelings), as well as the obvious objective meaning (events), the client is prepared for her reactions and feelings surrounding an event or situation. You have given the client the insight needed to change, or accept, the course of events. When you *absolutely let go* of outcomes and respect the life choices of others, you have empowered the client to grow in her own time and her own way. You have created the opportunity for your client to be the architect and author of her own life story.

It is important to emphasize that there is no such thing as "good" or "bad" tarot cards. They symbolize a spectrum of life experiences and *every* card presents an opportunity to learn and grow. Life brings change, with all its attending joys and sorrows. When people have a run of bad luck in their lives, they may be vulnerable to the suggestion of curses or hexes. Why is this happening? They want it to stop. Any reader who tries to turn their clients' fears against them (to make them more afraid) is out to control, rather than help, others.

Nothing in tarot is preordained. We always have the power to change trends through responsible choice. It is your duty as a reader to be honest. If you see a catastrophic event, such as loss of income or serious illness, you certainly need to be candid, but your role is to assist your client, not scare her to death. When catastrophe does strike, your client will be better prepared because you have helped her examine possible reactions to the situation ahead of time. A worthwhile tarot reading empowers your seeker to face any type of change with courage.

It is important for you to be up front with a client about your style of reading and state clearly what you can and cannot do. As a professional reader, you decide if you are a fortune-teller or guide. Putting oneself in the position of High Priestess with all the answers promotes dependency in clients, and makes you, the reader, responsible for the clients' actions. And who truly wants to be responsible for the decisions and actions of others?

Clients in Crisis

*In practical situations what you need to know is what
you need to know.
You need to know what to do. And that is all.*

— Wendell Johnson

People in crisis who would be threatened by a therapist or who simply can't afford one will often first go to a tarot reader, astrologer, or psychic. Clients in crisis are likely to be anxious, angry, depressed, confused, crying, or exercising poor judgment. They will ask for advice and be vulnerable to suggestions.

I believe there are two types of people who have a tarot reading during times of crisis: the spiritually aware souls who see cosmic implications to their predicaments and wish to learn from them, and the dependent souls who want to blame the universe for their circumstances and be told what to do. The second type of client is much more common than the first.

The term "codependent" originally came from the field of chemical dependency, but it is no longer limited to the families of alcoholics or addicts.[5] Literally, anyone who becomes "addicted" to another person, for any reason, and can't let go of the other person is exhibiting codependent behavior. For example, a client may become "addicted" to the advice of a tarot reader, psychic, or astrologer. Likewise, a tarot reader who is "addicted" to giving advice and controlling outcomes is codependent. Any person who becomes emotionally dependent upon another human being, is obsessed with the relationship, or wants to control the relationship to the point of having no peace of mind, is codependent.

Clients are particularly sensitive to a reader's underlying attitudes of blame, shame, or judgment. Many people blame victims for what happened to them and tarot readers are not exempt from this tendency. There is especially a New Age tendency to blame people for what happens to them—that somehow a rape victim caused the rape because of past karmic debt, for instance. This kind of talk does not help when the victim is contemplating suicide because it is another way of telling the victim that she somehow "asked" to be raped and reinforces feelings of shame.

Blaming the victim for a situation can help the reader feel more powerful or in control, because it is a way of dealing with the frustration of not knowing how to help the client in time of crisis. It also takes on the nasty quality of superiority: If the victim had been able to think only in positive terms (like the reader), this would never have happened in the first place. Shame, blame, and judgment have no place in a tarot reading because it is not helpful to the client in any way whatsoever.

Please note: Assisting a client to take personal responsibility for her life through insight is a positive, loving action devoid of shame, blame, or judgment. Think of yourself as a midwife to the psyche—you don't actually birth the baby, but you are there to ease the way.

A professional reader's ability to help a client is limited by many factors and the client's problems are often not within the scope of a tarot reading. The professional reader is able to distinguish between a stressful situation and a true emergency, such as the threat of suicide. The next section focuses on recognizing a true crisis, maintaining a state of calm, knowing what to do, and keeping a list of healthcare resources close by, including emergency numbers.

Before we go to crisis mode, however, we need to answer one big question: What in the world is a "normal" crisis? Every day presents a new opportunity for things and people to break down, but we get up, dust ourselves off, and eventually start over again. "Normal" crises are stressful but predictable events in life. They evoke anxiety and require adjustments, but are not pathological. People return to full functioning within a relatively short period of time. Examples of a normal crisis include moving, changing jobs, marriage, divorce, going to college or back to school after an absence, children leaving home, and menopause.

Please understand that, regardless of the actual severity of the situation, an emergency is perceived as serious to the person involved, and anxiety is its cardinal feature. Perhaps some current event is stirring up past fears. People are seldom aware of the specific fear, but are aware of diffuse panic or dread. Whatever the cause, past or present, people can become terrified that they are losing control of their lives.

Note: The only "true" psychiatric emergency is the threat of harming self or harming others. Please refer to "At-Risk Callers" in chapter 3 for ways to assess the urgency. Without exception, if our client is contemplating harming herself or others, we stop the reading and tell her to go to the emergency room, especially if she has a plan for carrying out such a threat. We also give her the toll-free number of the suicide prevention hotline and call 911 on her behalf if we sense real danger. It is not up to us to decide whether or not the threat is real. We leave that to people trained to handle psychiatric emergencies.

Emergencies come in all shapes and sizes, but with the overriding feature of anxiety, it is up to us to try to determine why this event has taken place *now*. Remember that we, as readers, may not think things sound so bad, but if our client perceives a crisis, it is a crisis. It is a huge disservice to trivialize or minimize another person's perceived pain or stress.

Identifying the precipitating event that brought our client to us can help us respond with compassion and intelligence. Even a common-sense answer such as "they didn't want more responsibility" or "they are afraid of losing the house" can help bring sense to a crisis. Bringing order to a stressful encounter reduces the fear that can paralyze the one standing at the center of the crisis. We can make things much worse by extravagant or emotional interventions. Now is not the time to get high off the fumes of an emergency. We decrease the intensity of the crisis by remaining calm and being a steady presence in an unsteady situation. We accomplish this by having control of our own reactions. Hysteria helps no one.

In order to remain calm during a crisis, I recommend thinking through an emergency plan and writing it out. When you sense things are spinning out of control or that the client's problems are outside the scope of a tarot reading, refer to your written plan of action. The written plan should include ways to evaluate a crisis, emotional first aid, knowing when to make a referral, motivating a client to seek outside help, and what to do when the client resists suggestions.

None of what follows is an all-inclusive list because I don't have all the answers. My suggestions are basic and designed to get you moving in the right direction. As you study and gain experience, incorporate your own plan of action during a crisis.

Evaluating a Crisis

Asking the right questions can help you distinguish between a stressful situation and a true emergency. The following questions can shed light on real or perceived threats to security:[6] Is anyone in actual danger? Does anyone close to the client pose a real threat? What is the worst thing that can happen? What are possible options? What resources are available? Is the client talking of harming herself or another? (Heads up!) Who is involved in this crisis and in what way? Is there a significant other in the client's life who can offer support? Does the client have a plan of action to alleviate this crisis? What has the client already done in reaction to this situation? How has the client reacted to similar situations in the past?

Calming a Client in Crisis

The main purpose of calming someone in crisis is to get more information so that you can make appropriate decisions. Sometimes a person will calm down if we allow them to talk while we maintain a respectful silence. We can validate, rather than diminish, feelings by saying, "Yes, this is bad." Letting someone know that we are listening goes a long way to soothe nerves and reinstate calm.

We can ask the person to breathe deeply with us before we continue with our questions. This is not a silly waste of time. People in crisis often have shallow, rapid respirations and they aren't getting enough oxygen to think clearly. Deep breathing restores balance by increasing oxygen flow to the brain.

People in crisis may also be in the excited "fight or flight" state:[7] the heart and respiratory rates, blood pressure, and blood flow to muscles are increased. This is the body's way of preparing for an emergency. Breathing too fast can cause hyperventilation—blowing off too much carbon dioxide—and low carbon dioxide levels leads to fainting.

If your client feels faint, have her breathe deeply into a paper bag for a minute or so to replenish carbon dioxide levels and prevent fainting. When you have no paper bag, there is a simpler technique that works as well: Have your client hold one nostril shut while breathing through the other nostril with her mouth closed until the faint feeling has passed.[8] Other calming options include giving flower essences such as Bach's Rescue Remedy or offering calming herbal teas such as chamomile. Do anything that you feel will decrease chaos, buy time, and promote calm.

Knowing When to Make a Referral

Referrals aren't as easy to make as you might think. Some readers may feel they are abandoning their client, or that a referral implies the reader is incompetent. Repeat after me: *A good referral is neither abandonment nor a sign of inadequacy when it is an honest recommendation in the client's best interest.*[9]

During a crisis, people are often more open to seeking outside help. Your familiarity with outside resources is reassuring to the client, especially when your client thinks there is no way out. Sometimes just shedding new light on a situation or posing another way to look at things is all the client needs to calm down and think about what to do. We must tell the truth about the reasons for a referral. Manufactured reasons for a referral never hold up and a short statement of why you believe the referral is necessary takes very little time. A clear, honest explanation goes a long way toward offering real help.

One of the most common reasons for a referral is that the nature of the client's problems is out of the scope of a tarot reading. For example, your client needs psychotropic medication to stabilize her mood swings. Another reason to refer is that you feel the problem is out of your area of expertise. For instance, your client has post-traumatic stress disorder and you know very little about that condition.

Perhaps, despite the best effort on everyone's part, you and your client can't seem to get on the right track. The vibrations are all wrong. Sometimes your personalities don't match up well and it's as simple as that. It is also time to make a complimentary referral if either you or your client is moving away or you are going out of business. In fact, most therapeutic relationships end because of reality factors, like a change in finances, moving, or death, than for any other reasons.

Developing a Resource Network

As a professional, you do not want to look up the names and numbers of referrals at the last minute when your emotional client is staring at you from across the table. Building a file of the best persons or the best agencies takes time, reflection, and consultation with other professionals. It is helpful to develop relationships with a number of possible referrals in the community.[10]

I am not going to tell you what names or agencies you should have on your list. It will depend on your philosophy of life. Whether you prefer complementary therapies or you stay with spiritual advisers, energetic healers, Reiki practitioners, acupuncturists, herbalists, psychic diagnosticians, or astrologers is up to you. Likewise, it is your decision to include board-certified psychiatrists, medical specialists, and licensed independent psychologists or social workers. My own list of referrals is a mix of both traditional and nontraditional practitioners because I believe whatever works, works.

I do believe professional tarot readers need to be aware of hospitals with psychiatric facilities and community mental health clinics that accept referrals in their area. Contact the local medical and psychological societies to get such a list. When in doubt, suggest your client go to the hospital emergency room and have the ER's phone number on your list. Social workers can also be helpful because they work with families. Use the yellow pages of your local telephone book for initial contact numbers.

Every community has certain agencies that help people, some private, some run by the state. In Cincinnati, Women Helping Women addresses sexual assault, stalking, and child sexual abuse. Many cities offer services to women in crisis. Organizations such as Alcoholics Anonymous, drug treatment units, suicide prevention centers with telephone hotlines, HIV/AIDS counseling centers, or battered women's shelters are all useful in dealing with the various crises that come up in the work of a tarot counselor. Telephone books often display crisis numbers inside the front cover. Knowing the right agency to call at the moment of need equips us to make a truly helpful referral.

Also consider self-help groups in your area and information on the Internet. Self-help groups focus on peer support and consist of people who share a common experience. They offer information and support based on the sharing of that experience. Self-help groups cover a vast range of topics, such as alcoholism and substance abuse, working through sexual identity issues, living with an HIV-positive partner, developmental disabilities, codependency, chronic emotional and physical conditions, as well as specific events such as divorce, death of a child or life partner, surviving suicide, or loss of employment. Look in the community section of the Sunday newspaper for listings of self-help groups in your area. Many of these groups have toll-free phone numbers and websites.

The Internet is a helpful resource for almost any illness, condition, dysfunction, or situation. Use a search engine such as Yahoo.com or Go.com and key in the search word of your choice. Just as the word "web" denotes, one site has links to another, and those sites have links to others until you have uncovered a lot of data. The American Medical Association, the American Psychiatric Association, the American Psychological Association, and almost every other professional organization you can name have information links. These links provide resources and direction about a wide variety of problems.

If you're like me, you try to recommend helpful books on a range of topics. Browse bookstores or libraries and research online bookseller sites. Become familiar with what's available. There is a self-help book for almost every subject. As you educate yourself on the literature, develop a reading list on a variety of topics. You increase your ability to help your client when you can recommend a pertinent book with confidence.

Motivating a Client to Seek Outside Help

The most important questions you can ask yourself when making a referral are: What is the greatest good for everyone involved? What is the best thing for my client at this time? Your client may exclaim, "But you're the only one who understands me!" As flattering as that statement may be, we need to resist the temptation to stay in a relationship that isn't for the highest good of all.

We can approach the client with skill and sensitivity by thanking her for the vote of confidence, but firmly stating a referral is in her best interest. We should avoid wasting time by spending hours talking about the problem. This focuses on the problem. Instead, we need to concentrate on possible actions because this focuses on the solution. Clients may not understand the choices available to them. Our knowledge of various resources is convincing because support and encouragement to seek specific outside help can strengthen the client's will to change.

The process of referral is completed when we step outside the picture, making it clear that we are no longer responsible for advice and counseling on this particular problem. It is very important at this phase that we avoid taking back responsibility.[11] If we reengage, we may be drawn deeper into our client's problems, and these were the problems we didn't feel equipped to address in the first place. Please resist the impulse to continue working on the same set of circumstances.

I once had an appointment to read for a woman who had eight children. She was pregnant again, at the age of forty-two, and came to me for a reading about the "karmic implications" of having another baby so close to midlife. She casually added that her physician had advised her against future pregnancies.

Since she was in the first trimester of pregnancy, I knew she didn't have sufficient time to contemplate her condition, but she seemed overly anxious, almost afraid. My first question to her was, "What brought you to a reading *today*?" Her response startled me: "Well, I am having light bleeding and abdominal cramps. I am wondering what the universe is trying to tell me."

It didn't take a tarot reading to figure it out. My twenty years as a registered nurse came into play, but anyone who had experience with pregnancy would have responded the same way. I instructed her to call her obstetrician immediately because she was having serious symptoms that could endanger her life and the life of her baby. Regardless of any karmic implications, her body was trying to tell her to get help. It was more important for her at this moment to seek professional health care than to have a tarot reading.

I could tell she wasn't satisfied with the answer and I wasn't sure how to connect with her, to speak the same language. I added that maybe the universe had sent her to a registered nurse on purpose. She then became more open to my suggestions because she believed that "there are no accidents." She called her doctor from my phone and left the bookstore to go directly to his office. A few weeks later, she phoned to tell me that she had been in the process of miscarrying and my early intervention probably saved her from hemorrhage.

I appreciated her follow-up call because not many clients take the time to do it. Mostly, I never hear the results of my referrals and maybe that's the way it is meant to be. I don't need to be reassured by outcomes to do my job. She never did have a reading with me, but I know I gave her the best I had to offer on that particular day.

It is a common professional practice in the counseling fields to send a note or make a call to the individual or agency chosen for referral. It is also a good practice to have the client's written permission to do so. Decide whether to make a call or get written permission on a case-by-case basis. In the example above, I did neither because she made the call. In the final analysis, it is always the responsibility of the client, the one being referred, to initiate contact or make an appointment with the new helper—which, of course, brings us to the last consideration.

When the Client Resists Suggestions

We need to assess client readiness to accept a referral and sometimes our suggestions will fall on deaf ears. Please don't take this rejection as a personal affront. Sometimes our clients will resist all forms of help and it has nothing to do with the quality of our suggestions. Even if a solution looks obvious to us, we are not the authors of our client's life story. People resist treatment in order to stay the same. Please keep in mind that whatever defense your client has against change is *exactly* the defense that is keeping her sane, or at least functional.

In other words, people resist treatment in order to keep functioning, however dysfunctional it looks to you. They also resist treatment to keep anxiety at bay by preventing awareness of a problem. Or, as I wrote in *Tarot for the Healing Heart*, maybe your client has the compulsion to repeat punishing behaviors by refusing to give up painful symptoms.[12] Your client could also like the secondary gain of being sick because she doesn't want to give up the attention and freedom from responsibility that her illness brings.

Resistant individuals do not want any changes to occur because any rearrangement of the dynamics may cause them to crumble and fall apart. They hold on to old ways of acting and believing for a reason: Whatever defenses they have, however crippling, helps them adjust to life. Maybe their solution is not ideal, but at least they can hold themselves together and cope to some extent.

So how do you know when your client is resisting your suggestions for help? It is rarely as obvious as a direct, "No, I don't want to do that." Your client may get angry with you and create a scene to deflect the referral, or your client may become a motormouth and not let you get a word in edgewise. Other tactics include laughing and making jokes, treating everything lightly (blowing it off, if you will), even if the situation is grave.[13]

Another clue that your client is resistant is if she speaks with great clarity about an emotional subject but shows no emotion. This is called intellectualizing.[14] If she speaks only about emotion but can't give specific details of her life, she is generalizing.[15] You can bet your client is generalizing if she makes blanket angry statements, such as "All women are cruel," but can't give specific examples of the cruelty. Finally, your client may try to resist referral by playing to your ego. We all like to be stroked, and being told how wonderful we are as readers is seductive. The earlier remark, "But you're the only one who understands me!" is an example of complimentary, seductive resistance.

Resistance to help is a defense against pain that cannot, and should not, be easily torn down. Never attack resistance to change by saying something like, "What's the matter with you? Can't you see what you need to do? It's so obvious!" It may be obvious to everyone but your client. She is in the dark for a reason and her survival may be at stake. Anyway, who are we to judge her soul-work and life lessons?

Each of us must decide if we want to keep the door open to this person for future contact. I can't answer that for you. We readers allow the resistance to stay in place because we are not qualified to blow the lid off defenses that are keeping our clients sane. We can understand the client's feelings about resisting help, but our "approval" is not necessary. All we need to understand is that we cannot, and should not, "fix" people. As professional readers, we respect life choices and let go, even if that means discontinuing the service for the highest good of you and your client.

The Ten-Minute Reader

A few years ago, I agreed to read the cards at a weekend holiday street festival from 12 A.M. to 12 P.M. Little did I know that the festival attracted over ten thousand people during the course of three days. My instructions were clear: Read for as many people as possible, with no reading to exceed ten minutes. The experience proved nightmarish for me because I didn't know how to take care of myself during reading marathons, and I wasn't used to quickie readings. I ended up with a bad case of sunburn and felt ill most of the weekend. I have since learned a lot about the special needs of all-day readers and I pass these tips for endurance on to you.

First and foremost, take care of your body and mind. If you are reading on a hot day in the sun, wear protective clothing, a hat, and use sunscreen. Keep a spritzer bottle of water nearby to cool yourself off on a hot day. Spray your neck and extremities often. Don't wear black because it absorbs heat. Drink plenty of fluid, eat easily digestible food, and take breaks. Drinks sweetened with sugar make you thirstier. Use beverages with caffeine or alcohol with caution because they dehydrate your body.

I don't read for more than fifty minutes at one time now. If I find myself in an all-day read-a-thon, I get up and walk around for ten minutes out of every hour. I stretch, go to the bathroom, get something to drink, or whatever it takes to get my feet back underneath me.

I believe in quality over quantity. I once declined an invitation to read at a festival because one of the written conditions was "No par-

ticipant shall leave or take a break without the permission of the orga-
nizer." Sorry, I'm an adult. I have the right to do what I need to do to
keep my sanity and take care of me. So do you.

I carry two boji stones in my pocket for grounding and an amethyst
for spiritual connection. I know of some readers who anoint their
throat, third-eye, and crown chakras with moldavite oil to aid in
alignment with the Higher Self. I'd like to think I have my head in the
clouds with my feet planted firmly on Mother Earth, but I am a Cancer Moon with a lot of Twelfth House stuff. I have a tendency to go
"out there" if I don't watch it. During my breaks, I concentrate on
grounding.

I have also learned to protect myself from negative energies when
reading in a crowd by visualizing a bubble of white and purple light
around me. I say a prayer and ask that only positive energy comes
through, while negative energy is harmlessly deflected back into the
earth. (I don't send negative energy back to its owner. Instead I envision
rose-colored light all around the individual, but that's a personal choice.
Kill 'em with kindness, I always say . . .) Other possibilities include
wearing crystals or protective stones, such as smoky quartz or jade, and
anointing your chakras with protection oil, such as sandalwood.

How you take care of your mind and body is entirely up to you. We
all incorporate customs into our practice based on our own spiritual
traditions. I can only tell you what has worked for me. The important
thing is that you *do* take care of your mind and body in some way
when reading the cards for long periods of time.

Now we turn to the tricky task of reading in ten minutes or less.
How can we start and stop a sample reading with grace and style? I
believe the key to success is finding an effective focus for the short
reading. The most popular topics for a tarot reading are love/relation-
ships, work/career/school, and money. Other common concerns are
the future, health, sexuality, spirituality, and past-life events. The overriding theme in all of these subjects is personal security.

When I give short readings, I am up-front about the length of time I
will spend on the reading. I usually say something like: "Think of this

ten-minute reading as a quick snapshot of your life, not a panoramic view. We won't be able to get into much detail but hopefully you'll enjoy the experience. Do you want a general reading or is there one area you'd particularly like to focus on?" Nine times out of ten, people come to the reading with a particular concern in mind and you have found your focus. If no specific concern is voiced, your focus is on the general meaning of the cards (and any intuitive insights that flash through, of course).

Regardless of whether the reading is general or specific, I do a three-card spread of past, present, and future. In a three-card spread with a particular focus, the past is what the seeker brings to the situation, the present is the nature of the situation as it is now, and the future looks at how events might unfold given the current circumstances.

A three-card spread is also effective for quick general readings, where the past is what the seeker brings to the moment, the present is a snapshot of today, and the future is a potential upcoming theme, if nothing about today changes. Use any small layout that appeals to you. Even one-card readings can be enlightening and fun. I don't use a larger spread because I can't cover too many cards in ten minutes or less.

When the allotted time has passed, I say: "Our time together is up. Thank you for having a reading with me today." And here's the key: I stop reading! I urge you to have good personal boundaries and stop reading when the time is up, or you'll find yourself giving thirty-minute readings for ten bucks.

Consider carrying business cards or brochures with you to encourage future contact. You might add something like: "In case you'd like an in-depth reading at another time, feel free to take my business card (or brochure) with you. Please call to make an appointment. Don't forget to tell a friend because word-of-mouth referrals are my best advertisement. Thanks again."

Another little trick I use is turning my business cards into refrigerator magnets. This can be done at very low cost by simply buying the magnets at an office supply store and gluing the cards on at home.

Most magnets are now self-adhesive—peel off the paper and stick your business card onto them. These make wonderful gifts at the end of a quick reading, or any reading for that matter. Business card magnets encourage people to keep you in mind because they place your card where they see it every day.

You have just read one woman's opinion on short readings done in quick succession. You can decide if you're going to offer general or specific readings and determine the layout you think would work the best for you. I think short readings are a specialized art form in tarot and they require incredible stamina. With a little care and planning, you can offer ten-minute readings with grace and style—and live through it to read another day.

Myths and Mermaids

"Once upon a time . . ." With these words, the power of story comes alive for youngsters whose imaginations are the doorway to identity and meaning in life. Whether by book or video, the myths of childhood can be a healthy aspect of development. These same myths can also create real problems, especially for girls.[16] Never forget, as a reader, you are weaving a story with the tarot cards that can have powerful implications for your teen seeker.

Today's teens live in a complicated world of cultural myths.[17] While most kids are healthy and well adjusted, all teens are bombarded with media messages promoting beauty over brains and feminine wiles over authentic self-esteem. Let's look for a moment at a beloved fairy tale that has been liberally changed and animated by Disney Studios. Based on a story by Hans Christian Andersen, *The Little Mermaid* is a classic example of an age-old formula: a maiden without a mother finds meaning in her life only through a man.[18]

This particular myth is a metaphor for a culture that promotes loss of self in pursuit of beauty, boys, and being nice. Advertisers present images of young women with bodies that are nearly impossible to achieve. There is such a high demand for the perfect look or the perfect face that the inner self is lost. Magazine covers display headlines for ways to get and keep boys, while the lyrics to some pop music screech that sexual abstinence is a liability.

Television, movies, and other media promote values that are in conflict with the wisdom of caring adults in teenagers' lives. The high incidence of eating disorders, depression, and low self-esteem is proof that many girls today buy into the myths of the culture. They sleep-walk through puberty into adulthood, and much like Sleeping Beauty, lay comatose waiting for Prince Charming to awaken them.

I am sensitive to the myths of teen girls because I struggled with anorexia nervosa for almost twenty years. As a teen, I was "nice," "the best," and valedictorian of my high school class. I was also a very sick puppy. Even into middle age, the myths I learned as a teenage girl still pollute the image I have of myself as a woman. I must be vigilant when I read for women, especially young women, or some of my prejudices spew forth into the reading. I am quite capable of "inflicting a reading" onto some unsuspecting soul.

In order to avoid polluting a teen's reading with personal issues, it is important for us, as readers, to confront our own attitudes about adolescence and examine unresolved conflicts about those years. For me, the examination will be a lifelong process. Reading the tarot for a minor is rewarding and beneficial if done well, and challenging and harmful if done with an air of disregard.

Please also keep today's world in mind as you read for teens, male or female. Focusing on current situations can help a teen learn about life situations that carry over into adulthood. If teens can use the information in a tarot reading to gain insight into how to handle today's problems, they will have the tools to approach adult difficulties as well—and that outcome of reading the tarot cards for teens is a service well done.

Communication is most effective when we are respectful and take all teen matters seriously. We need to remember how dramatic the teen years are and not minimize any concern. If we are viewed as an adult authority figure, the teen will be as thrilled with us as she is going to see a psychiatrist or school counselor. The challenge of the professional reader is to establish rapport and focus on the teen's concerns without coming across as a parental figure.[19] We can open the dialogue by talking about important teen matters, such as school, dating, or friends.

I do not believe it is wise to predict the future when reading for a teenager. Teens are not that focused on the future except in romantic and unrealistic ways.[20] For example, dreams of becoming a movie star have a purpose in the teen years and hope or motivation can be stifled if too much attention is given to the future, especially in negative ways ("I don't see any stardom in the cards for you . . ."). We readers should never dash the aspirations of an adolescent. Words have power and teens are vulnerable to suggestions. Given an adolescent's natural talent for drama, a doom-and-gloom prediction may be acted out in a type of self-fulfilling prophecy.

As with all clients, we readers need to honor teen confidentiality, otherwise there is no real communication. However, if a minor tells us something that is potentially life threatening, such as having thoughts of suicide, we have a legal and moral responsibility to notify authorities or we may be held liable.[21]

Liability for a professional reader is not held to the standard of a licensed trained healthcare provider and incidences of a reader's liability are rare. But here is an important disclaimer: Any adult who is being paid for a "consulting" service can still be held accountable for not taking action on information that could have saved the teen's life. The legal term for this inaction is "depraved indifference," with the literal translation being immoral or shameful apathy.[22]

Let's discuss Mom and Dad for a minute. If a parent requests that you read for her teen, it is vital for you to assess the parent's motivations. You need to stay away from anything that sounds like, "Here, fix my child," or "Please talk some sense into my daughter." You should avoid a request that comes out of the need to control an adolescent, but if it comes from a genuine and heartfelt wish to help, a reading can be of great benefit to a teenager regardless who requested it.

Another consideration for the professional is whether or not the minor is having a reading against the wishes of a parent. I read for a fifteen-year-old girl, *unaware* that her mother had forbidden her to have a reading. I later learned Mom thought the tarot cards were some form of Satan worship. I ended up with a screaming mother on the other end of the phone telling me I was leading her daughter into hell. While I never tried to argue with her, I did hang up—several times—before the calls finally stopped. It was most unpleasant and a profound learning experience for me. I have since simplified my life. Without exception, I no longer read for anyone under the age of eighteen.

You've looked at the counseling aspect of the cards and learned how to have grace under pressure when reading for a client in crisis. In the next chapter, you'll explore giving tarot to the next generation of enthusiasts through teaching.

6 ‖ Teaching—and Learning—Tarot

When the teacher *is ready, the students will appear.*

— Christine Jette

Teaching others how to read the tarot is creative, enjoyable, and down-right frightening, if not well prepared. It requires a commitment of time and energy. Adult learners want information that is accurate, concise, and immediately applicable. This chapter explores the keys to successful teaching with suggestions for organizing the class in a workshop format geared to the needs of adults.

There are many ways to organize and teach a tarot class. Every class reflects the personality and attitudes of its teacher. You will develop your class in a way that best meets the needs of your students and your environment. I can't tell you how to do that, but I can share with you my own philosophy and style of teaching. My outlines of a six-week beginning tarot course and a ten-week specialty course are found in appendix B, along with ideas for offering advanced classes. Whether you build upon them or not is your choice.

Starting with the section "Calling All Tarot Enthusiasts" to the end of the chapter, you will learn the qualities of an effective teacher and explore ways to evaluate a tarot instructor from the student's perspective. I do this to help you objectively look at your class through another set of eyes. My goal is to have this chapter serve as a launching place for your own growth and exploration as a teacher—and as a life-long learner. And for goodness sake, have fun!

The Workshop Format

Learning to read the tarot cards is like happiness—it's not a place to get to but a way to go. Each of us has a right to know joy at each level of growth. My intention for any class is to teach others how to learn. I subscribe to the old adage that if we give a fish, we have dinner; if we teach fishing, we eat for a lifetime. I want to teach fishing. I don't have all the answers and I learn much from my students when I am open to the exchange of ideas. I base my teaching style on the needs of adult learners: Adults want concise information that is immediately applicable and they want to direct their own learning.[1]

I use the workshop format of teaching in both my tarot and writing classes. The workshop is a forum where teacher and students become *partners* in the experience of learning.[2] A tarot workshop is more than a program designed to help students acquire the skills needed to read the cards. It is a classroom in which you and your students form bonds that become the foundation of learning. Your teaching becomes individualized as students focus on topics that matter to them and you respond to their efforts.

Every tarot workshop reflects the personality and attitudes of its teacher. You will develop your workshop in a way that best meets the needs of your students, time frame, teaching environment, and personal style. There are many variations of the workshop format. I will describe but one way to teach a tarot class. It is especially helpful when conducting a concentrated two- or three-day class over the course of one weekend because it allows for plenty of interaction, activity, and breaks.[3]

The model for my tarot weekend workshop starts with a ten-minute mini-lesson, which focuses on a skill or concept. After the mini-lesson, students work with the cards for twenty to twenty-five minutes. It is unlikely that all students will be doing the same thing. It's up to them to decide what is important. Your students may be involved with various activities, such as writing a tarot story, designing a layout, working with one suit, writing keyword "catch phrases" for each card, looking at the artwork, making an entry in the journal, or reading a suggested handout.

The entire classroom is used because activities are taking place with partners or in small groups. I make suggestions for activity and interaction, but I let my students decide what they want to learn and how they want to learn it. Some people need guided instruction while others want independence. No two workshops are ever the same.

During the class time, the workshop buzzes with a low level of productive noise. I circulate to check tarot progress, confer with individual students or groups, provide guidance, and answer questions. The last fifteen minutes of the hour is reserved for sharing, either individually or in groups. Students can take center stage and share with the entire class. When sharing with all the students, the rest of the class listens or asks questions. For small groups, students share with the members of their circle. Group members can then respond or ask questions. The only thing I insist upon is respect for differences of opinion.

As the weekend progresses, students gather more information; during the allotted work time, they may decide to concentrate on an earlier mini-lesson. For example, if we covered the major arcana in the morning and the court cards in the afternoon, a student may want to continue working with the majors later in the day. I leave all learning decisions up to my students because I believe we work on what we need to know. Here is the breakdown of a fifty-minute workshop hour, with ten minutes reserved for break:

Mini tarot lesson—10 minutes

Working with the cards—25 minutes

Sharing and questions—15 minutes

Another way to organize a tarot workshop is found in appendix B. I teach a six-week course, two hours each class. While I have taught the weekend marathon workshop, I prefer the six-week course because it allows students to work on their own time at home. I use the first fifty minutes as my "mini-lesson," we take a break, and in the last forty-five minutes I circulate while the students work on an activity that interests them from any topic of my mini-lesson. I leave the final fifteen minutes free for questions or comments.

As you can see from the description above, you are no longer the mere giver of information. As a workshop instructor, your new role is nurturer, facilitator, and promoter of learning. You will guide, encourage, and applaud students on their efforts. You will also help them discover new insights, make connections, analyze information, and communicate thoughts and feelings. You will give personal feedback that reinforces learning.

Aside from the mini-lessons, your time is spent working with individuals and small groups. Since modeling is a powerful motivator and teacher, on occasion you work with the cards right along with your students. And, of course, for the workshop to be successful, you give up any need to control learning or be the High Priestess. In this method of learning, you are more like the Hermit: shining a light to let others find their own way.

Some of you may worry that as you circulate around the room helping individuals, other students will stop working, or the workshop won't operate well with a large group. Perhaps you think some students will not have an opportunity to share. In my experience, a well-run workshop overcomes all these fears because students are involved in their own learning. Adults are self-directed learners and they get exactly what they need to get out of a workshop without much direction from the teacher.

Students are in your workshop because they chose to be in your workshop. They could be spending their time and money on something else, but they chose to spend it with you. If you are there to guide the way, adult learners will do the rest whether you worry about it or not. Because students focus on their interests, worries, and dreams when working with the cards, the material in a tarot workshop is the fabric of their lives. They already have all the motivation they need to learn about the tarot.

Working with the tarot is a powerful tool for learning. It enables us to analyze and synthesize our thoughts, feelings, and insights, while developing intuition. When we work with the tarot, we become conscious of ourselves and discover new ideas. We define ourselves and come to understand our lives. Through the tarot workshop, you will help your students begin to master the skills that will enable them to grow as individuals. I can't think of a greater goal for any teacher.

A Planning Guide

Every effective teacher thinks through the objectives of a class and makes lesson plans to reflect the goals. With clear goals in mind, this same teacher then lets go of the need to control outcomes and allows the adult class to progress in the way it wants to progress. You can use the following worksheet as a planning guide. It will help you develop and implement a well-organized tarot class.

- Describe your tarot philosophy in detail.

- What are the goals of the class?

- How much time are you willing to invest in preparation and teaching?

- What do you want to accomplish?

- What are the absolute essentials to cover? Describe your bare minimum.

- What are you willing to let go of if the class takes another direction from your original plan?

- What will be the structure or organization? (Majors first? Minors first? Court cards as part of the suits, or separately?) My own weekly structure is in appendix B.

- Will you use a tarot book in class, and if so, which one? Will you sell it or expect students to buy it on their own? Do you need to order books or notify a bookstore?

- Will you recommend a deck, and if so, which one?

- What kind of equipment will you need? Blackboard? Overhead? PowerPoint? Flip chart? Chalk, markers, erasers, pens?

- Will there be handouts? Do you have access to a photocopier?

- Consider copyright laws. Do you need permission from an author or publisher to photocopy? Are you giving full credit to an author if you are presenting ideas that are not your own?

- Where will the class be held (home, coffeehouse, office rental, Universalist church basement, community center, bookstore, library, etc.)?

- Is there plenty of parking and is the location safe?

- How long will the class be? Consider both the length of each class and the total number of classes involved. Allow for breaks.

- What day of the week and what time?

- Will you provide refreshments or are amenities available?

- Will it be in workshop format, didactic learning (teacher talks, students listen), class participation, or a combination?

- Who is your "ideal" student? Describe in detail.

- Who will be the target audience (from the ideal student above and chapter 2)?

- How many students make up the critical mass? In other words, how many students must you have to cover costs and your time?

- Are you willing to give private lessons, one-on-one? Will private lessons cost more? (I feel they should because you are devoting all your time and talents to one person.)

- Will you offer correspondence courses (tarot on the web or tarot by snail mail)? If so, how will the price and structure differ from the classroom setting?

- How will you advertise/market the class (flyers, newspapers, libraries, radio, bookstores, etc.)? Refer to chapter 2 for inexpensive ways to advertise.

- How much will you charge? Will you accept cash, check, or charge cards?

- Will you allow installment plans (pay as you go), or will you require the full amount during the first class?

- When and how will you issue refunds?

- Are you willing to answer questions by telephone during the week between class sessions? How available are you willing to be to your students?

- How will you notify people of a cancellation and will you make it up or issue a partial refund? (I suggest getting student contact information as soon as possible in case of emergencies.)

- Will you have the participants evaluate your teaching? How will you handle criticism? What can you learn from it?

First Impressions

First impressions are lasting. Think back to a class you attended that was taught by the absentminded professor. What type of impression did it make on you? Space cadet is not a complimentary term. We live in the age of improvisation and "winging it" is an accustomed way of doing things. We rationalize doing things without adequate preparation. Some of us speak of freshness and spontaneity, or playing it by ear, but that explains away carelessness rather than describing creativity.

I have noticed an especially peculiar belief that says creative persons are undisciplined and chaotic. Nothing is farther from the truth. The creative process may be chaotic, but creative people have an intense inner discipline that guides them in their work. The quality of what they produce is proof of their inner discipline.

Unorganized teaching produces only chaos. Organization is one of your keys to creative success and it begins before the first class. A little advanced planning goes a long way. Attending to the practical details a week or so before your first class will eliminate unnecessary sources of stress so that you make a fine first impression on your students.

- Double-check the time, date, and address of the class. Will you need to get keys from the owner? Make arrangements now. Plan to arrive at least a half-hour before class time so that you can set up and greet early students.

- Arrange for babysitters and transportation. Phone ahead for weekend or evening schedules for your bus, train, or subway. Calculate your travel time.

- Check the weather forecast twenty-four hours ahead of your class and on class day. Make a decision about cancellation as early as possible to allow time for notifying your students.

- Check your supplies now: your copy of the course outline, any handouts or decks you want to bring, small bills for change, machine to make credit card impressions, receipts, chalk, erasers, roster, sign-in sheet, flipchart, markers, and so on. Replenish anything that is low before the first class.

- Make a list of everything—*everything*—that you have to take with you. Then post it where you will see it on your way out the door and check it as you leave.

• Choose your clothes with an eye for comfort and confidence. Fashion is nice, but secondary. If you feel good, you'll look good.

Butterflies and Spinning Rooms

It's here. Tonight you are teaching your very first tarot class. You are about to go on center stage and you think you are about to throw up. Of course, not everyone will be nervous about getting up in front of a group of strangers. Some people thrive in the limelight. If you fall into this category, count your blessings. Most of us suffer from "stage fright" when all eyes are on us. A few simple steps will help make your first experience with teaching a good one:

1. Keep this day as stress-free as possible. Do whatever it is you need to do to stay grounded. Rest, eat, exercise, and review your notes. No one else's agenda will be exactly right for you. Avoid anyone who will undermine your confidence with comments such as "What's the big deal? It's just a stupid little tarot class." Welcome the support of your allies and let them help you.

2. Eat lightly. Anxiety interrupts the body's digestive function.[4] Heavy foods can give you a lump in your belly to go with the one in your throat. Avoid fatty foods such as butter, dips, mayonnaise, or chocolate because they will make your digestive system even more sluggish. Minimize your sugar intake but stick to your customary level of caffeine to avoid a caffeine withdrawal headache. Any low-fat protein will energize you and sharpen your responses. Try low-fat yogurt, cottage cheese, shrimp, or milk. Carbohydrates alone, without fats, are calming. Try crackers, plain toast, a muffin, or dry cereal.

3. Enjoy your talismans and good-luck charms. I won't go anywhere without a crystal pendulum in my pocket. I don't feel completely dressed without it. When I teach, I always wear my astrological pendant with its birthstone. I feel more balanced and integrated

with it close to my heart. Use or carry anything that has special meaning to you and gives you peace or confidence.

4. Don't fight your anxiety. The first thing I say to my class is "Thank you for being here. I'm a little nervous so please bear with me." My class appreciates the honesty. You don't have to cover up anxiety, repress it, or apologize for it. Do you remember how you felt when you were a kid just before a major holiday? The fluttery stomach, breathlessness, spinning rooms, or wobbly knees were pure excitement—and the physical symptoms are identical to performance anxiety. The physical symptoms of anxiety might appear hours before your class or they might not hit until your first student arrives. When you become aware of physical symptoms, work on any emergency measures that you know for calming yourself.

5. I am an amateur musician and I perform on a regular basis in a community concert band. I'm never going to be a professional musician. I make music because I love making it, but that doesn't stop butterflies or spinning rooms right before a concert, especially if there is a large audience. When you are a teacher standing in front of a room full of strangers who have paid you money, you are performing—and your performance is being evaluated, whether you think of yourself as a performer or not. Here are some suggestions from the pros on how to decrease performance anxiety:[5]

   • Anxiety changes our breathing patterns, either by producing shallow respirations or gulping in air. Don't breathe deeply now. It's too easy to hyperventilate and make yourself dizzy. Instead, *exhale*, blowing slowly through your lips until your lungs feel completely empty. As long as you make slow exhalations, the inhalations will take care of themselves.

   • Use any "calming breath" technique that you know from yoga or meditation.

- Release tension with loose, gentle movements. Short-circuit the effects of adrenaline by aligning your body: Bend your knees very slightly, open your chest, and lengthen your spine. Feel grounded and solid from the waist down and buoyant and released from the waist up.

- Push the wall. Stand facing a wall and place both your hands flat against it about a foot apart, level with your shoulders. Now try to push the wall over. You are contracting your muscles and this decreases the production of adrenaline. If you have no wall, try another isometric exercise: Put your hands together in front of you with your elbows out and your fingertips up as in a prayer position. Push your hands together as you say the letter S like a hiss. Relax the muscles as you inhale and repeat.

- Smile. Anxiety affects muscle tension all over the body and it is most obvious in the face. Smiling disrupts the pattern of muscle tension and can redirect your emotional state. You don't need a wide, silly grin. A gentle smile or even a pleasant expression will do the trick.

Difficult Students: The Stuff No One Teaches You

Your goal as a teacher is to promote independent thought while maintaining an atmosphere that is conducive to learning. I have been teaching adults in nursing, writing, and the tarot for a long time now. The majority of adults are in a classroom because they want to be there and the ambience is fun, interactive, and supportive. But over the years, I have had my problem adult students. They fall into three categories that I have named the chatterbox, the naysayer, and the resident expert.

The Chatterbox

One of the most challenging students is the adult who is filled with enthusiasm and won't stop talking. They interject comments every chance they get, disrupting the flow of information. On one hand, chatterboxes are excited about the tarot and try to relate everything you say to their own lives. You don't want to put out the fire of enthusiasm. On the other hand, you need to quiet the chatter if anything is to be accomplished during class time.

I have two tricks for talkative, overeager students. I thank them very much for their enthusiasm or comments, and firmly say that we need to keep covering the material. I repeat the request as needed, and suggest they save comments for breaks or after class. Or, if other people can't get a word in edgewise, I say that all participants need the opportunity to share. If the student still won't be quiet, I stand beside her with my hand on her shoulder and proceed with the class. I call it my "hovering maneuver." This technique is intimidating to some, and should be used with caution, but it does have a subduing effect.

The Naysayer

At the beginning of the first class, I emphasize that we are to respect one another's differences. I rarely have to do anything else. On occasion I have the argumentative participant or one who cannot tolerate opinions that are different from her own. If a participant has been disrespectful or negative, I invite face-to-face student responses during class time. Peer feedback works wonders. I also speak privately with the individual about the need to respect others. In all the years I have taught, I have issued only one refund because I asked the student to leave. The class thanked me for it later because this troubled soul was destroying everyone's ability to concentrate.

If the negative comment is directed at another student, and not you, I urge you to take action. You have a responsibility to maintain respectful behavior in the classroom. You cannot change another person but you can offer the naysayer choices. For example, you can tell the individual that she can either offer an apology and the class goes on, or she may leave. It's her choice. By giving her options, you have returned to her the responsibility for civil behavior. You have allowed her to see that her behavior has consequences, without becoming angry or defensive or sounding like a parent. Adults want choices, not ultimatums.

The Resident Expert

Resident experts need to feel superior. Underneath the grandiosity, they have a fragile sense of self-esteem and are hypersensitive to evaluation. They anger easily when criticized and require excessive admiration from others. They also have unreasonable expectations of how they should be the center of attention and are unwilling to recognize the needs or feelings of others.

The resident expert is difficult to have in the classroom because she makes other people, including you, uncomfortable. If you sense a student is manipulating you, bet that you have a resident expert on hand. In psychiatry, the resident expert has a narcissistic personality disorder,[6] but you are there to teach a class, not formulate a diagnosis or offer therapy.

What happens when the resident expert tells you that you are wrong or she knows how to do it better? Remember, the last thing you want to do is criticize this individual, put her on the defensive, or evaluate her performance, because the resident expert is quick to anger and make a scene. Your only goal is to reach some sort of compromise with this troubled person so you can proceed with the class.

The best way to short-circuit the resident expert is to agree with her. For example, she tells you during class time that she knows more about the tarot than you do. Your cheerful response for everyone to hear: "You may know more about the tarot than I ever will, but I'm in a difficult position right now because I'm trying to teach this class and you're a student in it. I know it's a problem. If you're not happy with my level of expertise, I'd be happy to issue you a refund and I apologize if I misled you. Otherwise, let's move on despite my shortcomings."

Let's pretend the resident expert calls you something truly derogatory, such as "You are stupid" or "You're an incompetent teacher." (My nursing assistant students have called me both and more.) The first impulse is to get defensive or angry, but that solves nothing. No extolling of your virtues will convince your student that you are smart or competent. Your best response is: "Yes, I may be incompetent (or stupid) at times, but I am doing the best that I can right now. If my best is not good enough for you, perhaps you should withdraw from the class. If you decide to stay, please remember that I am doing the best that I can and that's all I can do. You decide what you want to do."

As with the naysayer, you have once again returned the responsibility of choice to the individual. You have agreed with your resident expert by parroting her exact phrasing back to her. In this case, she called me incompetent, so I said, "Yes, I may be incompetent at times, but ..." Use the *exact words* your expert used when phrasing your response. As hard as this communication technique is to do, you will defuse the situation because you haven't given the person any more verbal ammunition. How can she argue with you when you agree with her?

Remember, your goal is not to offer therapy, but to get the class moving again. In both these examples, everyone saves face because you didn't challenge her superiority and she is still the expert. By agreeing with her, you are now free to teach. Yes, it's tricky, and it takes a strong sense of self-esteem on your part, but it works.

Think of a plan now concerning the disruptive or disrespectful student. How will you quiet the chatterbox who monopolizes class time? What will you do when a participant belittles the work of others, especially yours? How will you proceed when one of your students dons the role of resident expert and takes exception to everything you say? Expect the unexpected. Thinking through communication strategies before class will save time and frustration later. Your students will thank you for it.

The Ultimate Strategy

No matter what happens in class, keep smiling, enjoy yourself, and— teach with abandon. Safety last. The balance between care and abandon is fragile, but when you find it, your adrenaline will give you an edge and a special depth to your teaching. Through it all, remember your purpose. Stay in touch with *why* you are teaching others about the cards you love so much.

If you doubt your ability as a tarot teacher, take a global view of your situation. In the scope of real time, what you are doing doesn't matter very much. Yet, in the grander scheme of things, you're sending out exactly the kind of energy and love that keeps the world sane. We can't order it on demand. It has to come, bit by bit, from courageous people like you who dare to give tarot to the next generation of enthusiasts.

Calling All Tarot Enthusiasts: Learning with a Teacher

Most tarot readers are self-taught some of the time, and some are self-taught all of the time. But many of us who have tried to learn reading the cards on our own end up agreeing on this: There are certain things about tarot cards you can learn in a book, and certain things about tarot cards you can't learn in a book.

Each of us has a unique learning style; we learn best when we learn in a way that suits our personal style. Think about your own learning style for a moment: Do you prefer teaching yourself or do you like to have a guide when learning something new? Do you learn best alone or do you benefit from a group setting? If you decide that you learn best with a guide, then this section is for you.

Little, if anything, is written for the tarot student in search of a teacher. What do you look for in a tarot teacher and how do you find one? The decision to take a tarot class isn't always simple because of expense, time, effort, and busy lives. Before committing to a class or private lessons, ask yourself: Are you willing to practice working with the cards on a regular basis? Are you patient? Can you accept gradual progress? What are your goals in studying the cards? If you're a true beginner, you may not know your goals yet, but beginning is a goal in itself, and some tarot teachers specialize in beginners.

So how do you find a tarot teacher? Word-of-mouth is one way. Tarot thrives in a social network: Tarot lovers know other tarot lovers and are (usually) happy to make recommendations. Read the notices and talk to the staff at New Age bookstores or shops. Check out classi-fied ads in the local New Age journal. Search the web. Spread the word that you are looking for a tarot class. As you consider the possibilities, remember that not all good readers are good teachers. Good teachers are out there, but it pays to investigate before you decide. Wherever you look, look for the best. Never settle for mediocrity because you are an amateur or "just a beginner." You deserve to take yourself seriously.

When you phone the prospective teacher, briefly explain your learn-ing goals. Make a list of some questions you'd like to discuss: What are her goals as a teacher? Do the teacher's goals match your own? Does the teacher follow any particular school of thought or approach to the cards? Some teachers follow a systemized method of instruction from a specific philosophy. If you are receptive to it, then you have a good match. But, if you, as a learner, work best in a flexible setting and like to be a partner, you will prefer a teacher with a more flexible approach—one who fits her teaching to the student, not the other way around.

What is her teaching experience? Experience alone is no guarantee of quality. If your prospect has been teaching for many years, listen for a corresponding openness to growth and change. A young or new teacher can be a delight if she teaches with an open and collaborative spirit. Please don't base your judgment on experience alone.

And for the trick question, ask her why is she teaching? As she answers, listen for a sense that the person loves the tarot, likes to see other people learn, and knows how to help make that happen. That's enough. Also ask questions about practical details. What times are the classes? How much do they cost? How are they paid? What is the pol-icy about missed sessions and refunds?

There's no such thing as an ideal teaching personality. We can learn from every type of teacher. When you evaluate your prospective teacher, listen to your intuition. Did you like her? Do you detect enthusiasm, a sense of humor, imagination, or any other quality you feel is necessary to your learning? Did she communicate clearly? Was she interested in your goals and needs? Did you find the kind of per-sonality you respond well to as a learner?

Classes Begin

You have found your teacher and are now taking a weekend workshop or a six-week course. To get the most out of the learning experience, practice working with the cards. If the purposes of your practice assignments are unclear, ask about them. Don't assume they are unimportant. If you don't understand, ask. Communicate with your teacher or she may never know she's not reaching you.

Have faith in your teacher's skill and your potential. Give it a real try before quitting. And finally, be patient with gradual progress. If you're a true beginner, you are not going to know the meanings of seventy-eight cards in one weekend. If you've read for a while, and your teacher suggests major changes in the way you interpret the cards, you might feel you are going backwards. Don't get discouraged. Eventually your own preferred style and voice will emerge based on your life experiences and frame of reference. Spend extra time on the parts of the tarot you enjoy, and for the rest of it, well, be patient. It will come.

Evaluating a Teacher

Let's pretend you have signed up for a six-week tarot course and you have just attended your first night of class. Your teacher bears the major responsibility of building rapport with her class. As you think about your first tarot class, conduct an informal evaluation of your experience:[7] Does the teacher help you feel at ease? Is the atmosphere calm? Does the teacher encourage questions and input? Does she treat you like an adult—with dignity and courtesy, not condescension?

A skillful teacher knows how to evaluate students without being discouraging. You should hear positive messages from the beginning. Does the teacher create a supportive environment? Something is wrong if you are going home from class feeling humiliated or belittled. Talk it over with your teacher if you can. If things don't improve by the end of the second class, ask for a refund and shop for another tarot teacher.

Does the teacher show you how to work with the cards? Be sure you are attending a class and not a performance. Is your teacher showing how or showing off? There's a big difference between a demonstration and a display. In the early stages, a savvy teacher will concentrate on things that you can do well immediately, such as sorting your cards into suits or putting the major arcana cards in order. This gives you the opportunity to succeed. The point of this type of instruction is to seek out the skills you already possess and draw you forward from there.

We've all had a teacher who made us feel vulnerable, stupid, or embarrassed. I was so afraid of one nursing instructor that I used to duck into the linen closet when I saw her coming down the hall. To this day, I can break into a sweat at the thought of her. While the chances of such a grim encounter are small with tarot instruction, you know you have met the teacher from hell if

- The teacher is chronically impatient. We all have our off days, but if impatience is the teacher's style, it is the teacher's problem, not the student's. Some reading difficulties, such as relating the cards to each other in a layout or building a good narrative, take a long time to learn. An effective teacher acknowledges even partial improvement.

- The teacher talks about results and not the process. "Your reading style is weak," and "Your layout is all wrong" are not helpful statements. At the very least, a student needs to know what steps to take to correct a specific problem. Learning the foundations of reading—weaving narrative, relating the cards to one another and real life, asking the right question, or creating layouts—is better still. This supports growth as a reader in the long run.

- There is no creativity in assignments. A teacher who uses only one approach doesn't adapt the learning to the student. Progressing doggedly through the assignments is not teaching. Granted, talented students will learn regardless of the quality of teaching, but "lockstep teaching" requires little input from the teacher and does not address the student's needs.

- Most of the teaching is by rote memorization or imitation. Rote memorization is a wonderful way to begin learning the cards, to give us a foundation so that we can expand and explore our skills. It gives us something to work with, but modeling has its limits. A steady diet of memorization and teacher imitation denies the learner a chance to be independent and develop her own style and voice.

- The teacher belittles the type of deck you want to use. A teacher does not have to share your taste in tarot decks, but there is no room in a respectful relationship for condescension. Even if a teacher does not like your choice in decks, it does not mean your deck has no value. It obviously does to you. For continuity, she may ask students to use one type of deck for class exercises, but she is still obliged to respect your personal choice.

- The teacher encourages dependence and discourages initiative. The tarot lessons are for your benefit, not your teacher's. Your ideas, your contributions, and your questions are important. If you sense that they are unimportant, you have the wrong teacher.

- The teacher is unapproachable. A teacher who closes off communication before class, during breaks, or after class can also shut doors to learning about the tarot because she stifles enthusiasm. You have the right to ask questions. It's important to feel safe to express yourself—in words and through the tarot cards.

It's always worth the effort to try to improve a troubled relationship with direct communication. It's also important to admit that we may need to find another teacher. There's no point in blaming ourselves for a bad situation.

Sometimes, when we're trying to learn the tarot cards, we can fall into a trap that I call the "student syndrome": the feeling that we don't know anything and the teacher knows everything. We can avoid the student syndrome if we think of our teacher not as a parent (she will take care of me), or as a mechanic (she will tell me how these parts fit together), but as a travel agent. We welcome information, guidance, and assistance with the many small details, but it is finally our trip to make alone.

Empowering Yourself as a Student

As adult learners of the tarot, we may feel vulnerable or nervous when we find ourselves on the student side of a teacher-student relationship. We find it hard to do something well when someone else is hovering over us. As adults, we are used to being efficient, competent, and capable. Learning to read the tarot can call our grownup bluff: If we are to endure as readers, our desire to learn the cards has to be stronger than our need to appear competent.

For those of us who learn to read the cards out of a deep, personal desire, a tarot lesson becomes a time of laying our hearts open. The emotional turmoil we may feel as we try to learn the cards is a testament to the intensity and significance of the tarot itself. As tarot students, we can make the most of our classes if we

1. Put criticism in perspective. Many of us inflate the value of negative comments and dismiss praise. If we're paying a teacher to help us learn the tarot, we need to find a way to accept the teacher's observations and suggestions without feeling crushed, defensive, or skeptical. It's hard. Even the gentlest teacher can say something that strikes us as tactless or harsh. We might have to remind ourselves to listen to the caring spirit inside the message, or to put criticism in its proper perspective: It is just one person's opinion, after all, and has nothing to do with our worth.

2. Be willing to take risks. As tarot students, we have to risk being wrong, making mistakes, and sounding foolish during a reading or we will never grow. All a teacher has to work with is what we

bring to the class. It is to everyone's advantage to be bold, rather than fearful, when learning to read the cards.

3. Be an active learner. Think for yourself. As knowledgeable as teachers are, they may not be able to articulate their knowledge. You may have to teach yourself to read the cards by analyzing what your teacher says and asking questions. Being active means working out the solutions to our own problems. Even if our solutions are faulty, the effort we make is a learning experience. Being active also means doing our own listening as we read the cards. Letting the teacher do the listening is a habit we picked up in grade school. We turn to the teacher after a reading and ask, "How did I do?" as if we hadn't been there during the reading. A teacher is only a resource. Learning to read the tarot has to come from us.

You probably expect to see a fourth item here: practice, practice, and more practice. It's obvious you will learn to read the cards faster if you practice. What is less obvious is that tarot classes can be of great value even if you don't have the time to complete all the assignments. Class can still be a time of discovery, communication, and self-actualization, even if "progress" as a reader is minimal.

There is no point in students being ashamed or teachers being aggravated over the issue of incomplete exercises. Teachers can be overly enthusiastic and neglect to calculate the amount of practice time they are asking of you. You shouldn't have to be demoralized by taking home assignments that are larger than you can do. If your "homework" feels impossible, speak up.

Let's say you are practicing very little with the cards. You may value the lessons while the teacher thinks you are wasting her time and your money. Does that mean you should withdraw from the tarot class? Maybe not. Why not invent a relationship between student and teacher where being part of a tarot community, and not progress, is the objective? It's an honest question worth exploring with your tarot teacher.

The way into the world of tarot is rarely smooth or predictable. A relationship with a tarot teacher is a unique human bond. A good teacher will be a catalyst for your personal relationship to the cards. If you loved the tarot when you started your classes, you should love it more when the classes are over. It is the desire to learn and the joy you get from working with the cards that will endure.

Learning on Your Own

Can you teach yourself how to read the cards? Of course! Most of us do. Learning to read the cards on your own is especially good if you: like to figure things out for yourself; think of unexpected developments as side trips, rather than wrong turns; and enjoy making new discoveries while finding ways to use them. In addition, learning on your own is better suited to a hectic or busy schedule.

Learning on your own doesn't have to mean learning all alone, however. Reinforcement and encouragement are important in the beginning. Your most important allies are your own deck of cards, your intuition, and a journal. The next most important resource for self-taught readers is a community of other readers. You'll save yourself a lot of frustration if you have at least one sympathetic and competent reader you can turn to when you get stuck or have questions.

Other major resources for self-taught readers include tarot books, audiotapes, videotapes, and computer software. Most tarot magazines, tarot websites, and newsletters carry reviews of tarot books, decks, tapes, and CDs. You can also ask a friend or clerk in a New Age bookstore to recommend materials.

There are more self-instruction materials on the tarot market today than ever before. With so much to choose from, how do you evaluate the book, tape, CD, or system of learning? My first rule is to be skeptical—or at least realistic—about extravagant claims. Becoming a skilled reader takes time. A method that offers "ridiculously simple tarot" usually means just that—you learn uncomplicated definitions for the cards and do easy readings. Simple can be a wonderful way to begin, but common sense tells us not to expect anything more. We have enough experience with instant coffee and instant banking to know what instant tarot means: Something has been sacrificed, or at least postponed, in exchange for quick results.

Does the book or teaching method really start from scratch? A method that omits basic tarot information, such as deck structure or standard meanings of the cards, is not necessarily a bad choice, but it does mean you'll have to look elsewhere for additional help if you need it. Some books teach you how to read the cards and some books show you how others read the cards. The distinction is important at the beginning level.

A person who already knows how to read the cards can listen to a tape or read any book to pick up useful tips. We need models, of course, and we can learn a lot from the masters of the art. But a beginning "teach-yourself-tarot" method has to do much more than display a finished product, in this case a tarot spread with interpretations of the cards. It has to teach you how to get there step by step. Tarot is a journey, not a destination.

The quality of tarot materials is improving, so the medium you choose depends upon your own learning style, budget, and personal preferences. Books are cheaper than private lessons—but only if you use them. Just as a book will patiently repeat material to you, it will also patiently sit on your shelf, doing nothing. Any motivation to use self-instruction tarot books comes from you. Self-teaching may work for some learners, but for others, there is nothing quite as motivating as an appointment with a teacher or tarot group. You decide.

The Tarot Plateau

Progress in reading the cards, like learning any other new skill, is never completely smooth or gradual. For days, weeks, or months you may fly—you learn new layouts, the meaning of many cards, and expand your understanding of yourself at a dizzying pace. Then comes the plateau of learning: the days, weeks, and months when, no matter how hard you work, nothing seems to change; you get no new insights or the cards make no sense. You may even feel like you're going backwards. You knew the meanings of all the court cards last week. Why can't you remember them now?

The plateau of tarot is a time of integrating and absorbing what you have already learned and a way of preparing your mind, emotions, and spirit for the next great leap ahead. Think of a plateau as a time of gathering or harvesting, rather than growing. Early plateaus of tarot learning are discouraging because we have very little foundation to fall back on. During later plateaus, we can return to our foundation, rest, and enjoy our previous accomplishments. But if you're new to tarot and have few accomplishments behind you, the first plateau can be a real trial. I know one tarot expert who describes the three-lesson adult: the enthusiastic beginner who quits after three weeks. In tarot, we can quickly hit the wall of discouragement because there is so much to learn.

Plateaus can also occur when we have been working with the tarot for many years. The cards grow stale, we look for books to inspire us, and it feels like there isn't anything new under the sun. Tarot has lost its magic. I don't believe the cure for tarot apathy is finding new material, although an original thinker can certainly breathe a breath of fresh air into the literature. The problem isn't tarot; instead it is the way we look at the cards. We are better served if we change our angle, like the Hanged Man, and look at old information in new ways.

Keep plateaus in perspective and be ready to take good care of yourself when you're in the middle of one. Here are a few tactics for riding out the tarot plateaus. They can also help rekindle the flame of interest if you've been around tarot a while and feel it has nothing more to offer you.

- Spend extra time going deeper into material that you already understand. For example, if the Star intrigues you, write a poem or meditation for it, read more about it, or design your own card. Expanding upon your current knowledge of the tarot can ease the frustration of not understanding the rest of it. Reversals and court cards can wait. Get a firm grasp of what you do know.

- Don't let a tarot teacher push you faster than you are willing to go. Most sensitive teachers will offer encouragement and support if they know you are frustrated. Tell them. Often a teacher who sees you every other week for class will perceive results from your work with the cards that you have overlooked.

- Learn with friends. Organize a tarot support group that meets regularly to share layouts, card interpretations, and mutual encouragement. Find a phone buddy—someone you can call when you are stuck or discouraged.

- Find ways to have fun with the cards! Read by candlelight. Have a potluck-and-reading party. Use a tape recorder and tape your tarot journal entry instead of writing it. Listen to your recording. Throw a tarot costume party. Invent a tarot recipe book. What would the Queen of Cups eat for breakfast? In my second book, *Tarot for the Healing Heart,* I suggest ways to play with the tarot cards (pages 96–98). Use the suggestions to stimulate your own sense of play.

- Work hard on a challenging card, suit, or layout—then leave it alone for a while. When you return to it later, some difficulties will have been resolved because your unconscious was working on them while you were away. You will also bring a fresh perspective to the conundrums that remain.

- Sign up for and attend a tarot workshop or convention.

- Treat yourself to a new tarot book, a new deck, tarot software, or a journal subscription.

- Spend an afternoon in a bookstore or library browsing through tarot books, music, and decks. You don't have to buy anything, but it's fun to look.

- Find someone with whom you can share what you know. Read for a friend, even if it means you have your books wide open. Encourage a beginner.

- Pick a card a day and see how the day unfolds. At night, think about how your day related to the tarot card and make an entry in your journal.

- Never underestimate the power of gold stars. If you set a tarot goal for yourself and meet it, celebrate!

One definition of insanity is doing the same things over and over, expecting different results. You'll get through the frustration of tarot learning plateaus, or stagnation, if you find new ways to approach the cards. You don't have to ask yourself, "Am I learning anything?" or "Is there anything new to learn?" If you are working on it, interested in it, and doing your best, then you are learning—or learning anew.

The tarot works on us in mysterious ways and no matter where we are in our journey, we can never know all of what we are learning. But, rest assured, we are certainly learning more than we think. If we no longer find joy in the cards, we need to either put them away for a while or look for new approaches that inspire us. We have the surest sign that we are making the type of progress that matters most when we are touched and renewed by our work with the tarot.

In this chapter you examined tarot from the perspectives of both teacher and student. In the epilogue, you'll travel the road to psychic burnout and explore ways to maintain the energy to succeed.

Epilogue || The Energy to Succeed

The work of shaping the future consists not in the ruthless excision of everything and everyone standing in our way, but in the gentle returning of ourselves and our abilities to the pitch of our innate life's purpose.

— Caitlin Matthews

A healthy lifestyle is one of your most valuable professional tools. A clear mind produces a clear reading. Think of your body as the support system for your brain. Creativity thrives on good health: the healthier you are, the more your creative juices will flow. When you maintain good health, you have the energy to succeed, but helping others all day long can take its toll on your psyche. The epilogue focuses on help for the helper and begins by exploring the road to burnout.

The Road to Burnout

True or false:

___ Professional tarot reading feels like the perfect job.

___ Being in business for yourself is the solution to all your problems.

___ You would rather work than do anything else.

___ You are soaring with high hopes and expectations at the prospect of being a professional tarot reader.

___ You are a hard worker and give 110 percent to any job.

___ You are an idealistic, self-motivated achiever.

___ Anything is possible if you just work hard enough.

___ You're a perfectionist with high standards and expect others to be the same way.

If you answered true to any of the above statements, be wary. You're a candidate for burnout, a state of physical, emotional, and mental exhaustion caused by unrealistic expectations and impossible goals.[1] The road to burnout is paved with good intentions. There is nothing wrong with being idealistic, hardworking, self-motivated, or a perfectionist. There is also nothing wrong with having high aspirations, dreams, and goals. These are admirable traits. The villain is unreality: Unrealistic job aspirations and expectations are doomed to frustration and failure. The burnout candidate's personality keeps her striving with intensity until she crashes and burns.

Burnout progresses by stages that blend and merge into one another so smoothly that the victim seldom realizes what happened, even after it's over. At first, the job is wonderful and everything seems possible. Then you realize that your job as a self-employed tarot reader isn't all you thought it was cracked up to be. Something is wrong, but you don't know what. You work even harder to make your dreams come true. Working harder doesn't change anything and you become tired and frustrated. You start losing your self-confidence.

Early enthusiasm gives way to chronic fatigue and irritability. Eating and sleeping patterns change. There is a danger of binge behaviors, such as alcohol and drug use, binge eating, shopping sprees, or gambling. As you become more frustrated and angry, your work deteriorates and people start to notice. You are cynical and detached, beset with depression, anxiety, and physical illness. You start canceling or not showing up for appointments.

Despair is the dominant feature of full-scale burnout, as you experience an overwhelming sense of failure and loss of self-esteem.[2] This may take several months, but you feel alone and empty. You have a paralyzing "what's the use" pessimism about the future. You are exhausted, and physical and mental breakdowns are common here, including heart attack, stroke, and suicide. Here are a few indicators of stress that tell you it is time to get help *before* you experience full-scale burnout:[3]

- You feel trapped, like there's nowhere to turn.

- You worry excessively and can't concentrate.

- The way you feel affects your sleep, eating habits, job performance, relationships, and everyday life.

Just as the phoenix rises from the ashes, you, too, can rise from the ashes of burnout, but it takes time. If any of the burnout descriptions applies to you, it's time to interrupt this devastating process. First, you need to rest, relax, and break the cycle. Don't take your clients' problems home with you. Get away from your work for a while. During your time away, look at your job expectations, aspirations, and goals. Try to be realistic.

Talk to a trusted friend, adviser, or see a counselor, but be careful. Your readjusted aspirations and goals must belong to you, not someone else. Trying to do what someone else wants you to do is a recipe for continued frustration and burnout. Create balance in your life by investing more of yourself in family, personal relationships, social activities, and hobbies. When you spread yourself out in a more balanced way, your success or failure as a tarot reader won't have such an overpowering influence on your self-confidence and sense of worth.

Calgon, Take Me Away . . .

A wise saying informs us that an ounce of prevention is worth a pound of cure. Preventing burnout is easier than curing it. Humans once had to deal with life-or-death situations on a daily basis when they needed to protect themselves from predators. To assist us with quick action, our bodies coped with predatory danger by increasing our heartbeat, raising our blood pressure, tensing our muscles, and producing adrenalin.

Nowadays, we have modern predators: The feeling of being over-stressed occurs when we have difficulty handling the pressures of busy everyday living. Take the time today to plan a personal stress management program while you work toward your goals as a professional tarot reader.

Choose methods for stress reduction and relaxation that appeal to you. If it isn't fun, or at least enjoyable, you won't do it. It doesn't matter if you choose meditation, tai chi, hypnosis, biofeedback, bubble baths, visualization, a walk in the woods, swimming, jogging, bicycling, listening to music, playing a musical instrument, drawing, painting, writing poetry, caressing a cat or frolicking with your dog—as long as you like doing it.

Start with the basics: Are you getting enough sleep? Sleep deprivation affects our mood. If you're getting less than seven hours of sleep a night, you are sleep deprived. Is it a simple matter of turning off the late show and getting to bed earlier? Or do you need to see a health professional? Another simple remedy is eating right. Skipping meals, loading up on junk food, and forgetting to drink enough water are common reactions to stress, but they make it worse.

When we're under a lot of pressure, we need to keep our blood sugar stable and our digestive systems calm.[4] Try to eat regular, balanced meals and snacks. Take slow, deep breaths before eating and drink a glass of water. Turn to healthy foods that comfort you. When all else fails, try the beverage that got England through World War II—a beneficial cup of tea.

When I was younger, I practiced "better living through chemistry" and it came close to killing me. Substance abuse comes in three stages: fun, fun with problems, and problems. I am in no position to instruct anyone on lifestyle choices. We each must face our shadows in our own time, learn our own lessons, and find our own way. I can write with certainty, however, that excessive use of alcohol and drugs masks the feelings of stress for a short time, but they can't erase emotional or physical tension. Their use will not permanently fix any problem because recovery is an inside job. F. Scott Fitzgerald once told a friend that he didn't write better when he was drunk—he only thought he did.

Relying on caffeine to get us through the day leaves us in a bundle of nervous energy, not a relaxed state of mind. Cigarette smoking speeds up the heart, deprives the brain of oxygen, increases our risks for cancer or emphysema, and interferes with our natural ability to reduce stress. And it smells nasty when we are in close contact with our clients.

On the lighter side, try my favorite stress reduction technique: laugh every day. I have heard it said if we learn to laugh at ourselves, we will be amused for a lifetime. We take ourselves so seriously, yet life can be absurd, and we'd do well to laugh at the punch lines. Laughter releases endorphins (natural antistress chemicals in our brain), expands our lungs, exercises our belly muscles, and uses fewer facial muscles than frowning. A lively sense of humor is a common trait among healthy people.

Cultivate—or reawaken—your sense of humor. Only you know what tickles your funny bone. Here are a few things that work for me. Ask a child to tell you the latest joke that's going around school. Are you old enough to remember the Moby Grape jokes? Rent funny movies (I like Steve Martin, Robin Williams, and the humor of Tom Hanks), watch a comedy channel, read an amusing book, or call a friend and share something ridiculous. Read anything by the late Erma Bombeck. Watch reruns of *I Love Lucy*, *Seinfeld*, *Frasier*, or your favorite syndicated sitcom.

Listen to the remastered version of Bud Abbot and Lou Costello's "Who's on First?" Buy a George Carlin or Bill Cosby tape from the early part of their careers. "Growing Up Catholic," "The Seven Words You Can't Say on TV," "Child Birth," and "The Dentist" are especially funny (the first two are by Carlin, the latter two are by Cosby). Tune in to *Saturday Night Live* and catch a few cable episodes featuring the original cast. Take a friend to a comedy club show. See how much better laughter makes you feel. There is no cure for birth and death, so learn to enjoy the interval.

In a successful stress management program, you do something pleasurable on a regular basis; set aside time for yourself every day and do it with a commitment to your well-being. It doesn't have to take a lot of time—twenty minutes to a half-hour per day should do the trick. Nearly every stress reduction activity has immediate results, but you'll reap greater benefits if you start an activity and stay with it. You'll be more alert, feel emotionally balanced, and have the energy to succeed.

The Struggle for Meaning

Meaning comes before commitment. When we find meaning in our work, it is easy to make a commitment to it. Our work as professional tarot readers can lose meaning because it is draining to listen to people's problems all day long. When our work centers on people with problems, we become vulnerable to the loss of meaning. If we've been professional readers for a while, we may find ourselves heaving a sigh of relief when the day is done. Or worse, muttering that we no longer care: "Why am I doing this? These people are crazy!" Maintaining the commitment to help others takes a conscious effort on our part.

The meaning of our work as professional tarot readers is found in its human relationships and the quality of its human dimension. Yet, if we pursue work in any helping field, we may disconnect from the human dimension. We don the armor of disinterest to protect our own psyches. We need to learn to pursue meaning in our work as readers the way we pursue tarot expertise and knowledge of business—recognizing it for the resource that it is. To protect our work from the erosion of time, we may have to rediscover the core purpose and values that have motivated healers and advisers since the beginning: The meaning of reading the cards for someone else is not profit, but service.

Service is not a technique. It is a relationship, and it is more than a relationship between an expert with a pack of cards and a problem. Service is a human relationship. It is recognizing that we are working with individual human beings with souls, not cases, clients, or cards. There is another beating heart and spirit sitting across from us at the table, after all.

Service is, in my opinion, the most powerful antidote to cynicism, depression, and burnout so widespread in the helping professions today. As tarot readers, we are not trained to recognize meaning through service—yet there is a deep river of meaning that runs through our daily work as readers. Tapping into the wellspring of meaning through service is not complicated. Simple tools will offer us profound results.

Keeping a journal is the simplest tool to restore meaning to your work as a tarot reader. Make an entry at the end of the workday. Review your day backward by starting with the evening and ending with the moment you got out of bed. Do this three times. As you go through the events of your day the first time, ask yourself, "What surprised me today?" When you come to something that surprised you, write it down. Then start your review again and ask, "What moved or touched me today?" Write it down. The third time that you review your day, ask, "What inspired me today?" Make your final entry. It takes about fifteen minutes to write three entries for the things that surprised, moved, or inspired your day.

At first, you may not be able to answer these questions. The secret is to look at the day, not as a tarot reader, but as a writer, novelist, journalist, or poet. Look for the stories. In the beginning, you may find that you can see life only hours after it happens to you, that is, as you're making an entry in the journal. As the capacity to find meaning through service begins to grow, the gap between your life and the realizations about your life begins to narrow. And then the miracle occurs: One day you will realize that you are surprised, touched, and inspired at the very moment that life is happening, including your tarot consultation sessions.

I often wonder if meaning through service has an inverse relationship with expertise: The more we know, the more "successful" we are, or the more our reputation swells, the less meaning we have in our work. One of the worst readings I ever had came from a "world-renowned" psychic. She was robotic in her presentation and full of her own accomplishments. One of the best readings I ever had came from an enthusiastic beginner in New Orleans. She hadn't had time to become cynical, depressed, or to forget why she chose to read the cards for others in the first place.

As professional tarot readers, we must defend our sense of meaning in the service work we do. When we strengthen our sense of meaning against fatigue, numbness, overwork, or unreasonable expectations, we maintain our commitment to quality reading—and preserve the meaning in service for those who come after us.

Accepting Changes in Your Identity

Throughout this book, the basic tenet of professional tarot reading is informed choice for clients. Individuals (clients) make better decisions when they have information about the potential consequences of each possible course of action. And having made a choice, this advance information helps them anticipate what's coming and adapt to change with courage.

In the spirit of informed choice, learning to be a professional tarot reader, like learning to perform any new role, involves change—not only in what you know and what you do, but also in who you are. Who you are affects the professional tarot reader you will become, but this process is a two-way street: As you progress in your new career, your idea of who you are will also undergo change.

Change is the natural order of the universe, yet isn't it curious how hard we work sometimes to block it? We all know the doubters in our lives, the near and dear who bombard us with negative scenarios, however well-intentioned the comments may be: "I'm only telling you this for your own good," or "Do you really think this is practical?" When talking to others about your new life as a professional reader, ask yourself whether they are truly supportive of your efforts, or will they cast their own shadows of doubt and envy on your path?

Change and success produce varied and surprising effects. Even if you don't seem any different to yourself, others will perceive you differently, especially those in your social network. Your closest circle of friends probably encouraged you to become a professional reader or at least they support your ongoing efforts. But the "you" they encouraged is changing with the growth process. How will they respond to the new, more confident you?

Some people may become wary and exclaim, "Don't practice any of that tarot stuff on me!" Or you'll magically become the community counselor and people will try to seek your free advice. Probably the best you can do is to pay more attention to your strongest sources of support and maintain relationships with them. Watch for saboteurs who try to wound you with their negative talk. Do not tolerate anyone who wants to keep you the same. Share your dreams of becoming a professional tarot reader with only your allies—and know who they are.

Going Pro with Tarot

When we work with the counseling aspect of the tarot cards, we can know just enough to do a lot of harm to others and to ourselves. Operating solely on goodwill or the desire to be helpful does not make us competent to read the cards for money. True professionalism gives us a healthy sense of where we stand, what we know, and what we can—and cannot—do.

We need time for regular study. Some people who engage in reading the cards every day seldom consult tarot books or attend workshops.

Perhaps they feel that they know all there is to know about the tarot. No matter how much experience we have, it is always helpful to study the cards to expand our frame of reference because we are reading for other people in all walks of life.

A wise proverb reminds us that knowing others is wisdom, but knowing ourselves is enlightenment. All professionals go on learning throughout their lives. The desire to learn more through the use of the tarot is at the heart of being a professional reader.

One of the most remarkable things about reading the cards is that it works even when the reader is imperfect. Doing some of the right things in a reading makes up for doing a lot of the wrong things—and doing things right centers on letting go of the need to fix people or have all the answers. We need not worry or be ashamed of the truth that human beings make mistakes and errors will always be part of the human condition.

If, after all our best efforts, we feel that we do not function well as readers, there is nothing wrong in deciding that professional tarot reading is not for us. We do not claim to be professional tarot readers if we truly are not. Such a decision frees us to develop other talents and may reveal our better skills, and higher purpose, in healing, writing, astrology, spiritual advising, or any other path.

Professional tarot reading is a process that can assist those who choose to use it to become stronger and more capable. At best, professional tarot readers can help people find a greater measure of personal satisfaction in their world, clarify goals, and deepen their connection to the divine. At its heart, professional tarot reading assumes and respects the capability, integrity, and self-determination of all those who seek our services. What a worthwhile profession. Be proud of who you are and what you do.

Appendix A | The Professional Tarot Reader's Code of Ethics

When in doubt, be human.

— Karl Menninger

To view other versions of the tarot reader's code of ethics, please visit:

- Tarot 900, a code of ethics for 900-line readers. Address: www.geocities.com/RainForest/Canopy/1956/code.html

- The American Tarot Association's code of ethics. Address: www.ata-tarot.com/code.html

Diane Wilkes's Tarot Code of Ethics

I primarily use the tarot as a multi-level instrument to assess and explore your personal and professional concerns. Once we have delved into all aspects of your issue, we can determine potential actions and belief patterns that can serve as transformative, positive solutions.

My focus is not predictive, but I can't deny that the tarot is an oracle, as well as a tool for self-assessment and self-help. My method of reading is to concentrate on interpreting the cards, based on my years of study and my intuition. Any forecasting derives naturally from that point of convergence.

We're all blessed with free will, and a tarot reading provides a studio portrait of the future, based on matters remaining the same as they are at the time of the reading. If you don't like the photograph, you have the power to redo the picture to your personal satisfaction.

Tarot is a symbolic language. Each card has multiple potential meanings, depending on the surrounding cards. The Death card (No. 13) does not mean actual physical death. I translate the language of tarot, and work with you to achieve clarity, and a sense of preparedness and confidence, to face whatever issues have arisen. My role is to empower those who come to me for tarot readings, not scare you or assure you of my "powers."

I am a tarot reader,[1] not a doctor, lawyer, or financial advisor. I recommend that you seek professional advice on any medical, legal or financial matters. I will never offer to remove a curse or perform a magic spell for money. I urge you to avoid any tarot reader who offers these services to you. Scam artists reflect badly on legitimate, ethical tarot readers. REMEMBER: Just as there are bad doctors, there are bad tarot readers. I urge you to use common sense when choosing either.

It is my pleasure and my responsibility to treat every seeker with warmth, sensitivity, and compassion. I hold your tarot reading, and any information you reveal, in the strictest confidence. I am not entitled, nor do I want, to judge your past, present, and/or future actions. Any decisions that you choose to make based on the reading are your responsibility. Please do not see me as an oracle. The *tarot* is an oracle; I am the human interpreter, and as such, fallible. The tarot cards, like the planets, *impel*. They do not compel. *You* are the one who holds your future in your hands.[2]

Appendix B || Tarot Course Outlines

Art is a technique of communication.
 The image is the most complete technique of all
communication.

— Claus Oldenburg

A Sample Tarot Course

The following outline is the basic structure of my six-week tarot class. Classes are held every two weeks for two hours each meeting, with one break at the end of the first hour. The outline serves as a general organizational structure for reference. You'll find the format of *what* to cover Week 1, Week 2, Week 3, and so on, but not *how* to cover it. I leave all expressions of personal style and voice up to you. Think of it as a place to start. It is designed to stimulate your own creative processes.

In the first fifty minutes, I briefly cover topics found under the "Mini-Lesson" heading. Of most importance, *adults direct their own learning*; as workshop instructor, I have given up any need to control learning. Because I use Mary K. Greer's *Tarot for Your Self* as the basic text, and give my students a large notebook filled with many informative handouts to read at home, I do not try to cover each topic in detail. Rather, I teach them how to learn more about each topic, where to find the information *on their own*. After a ten-minute break, the students spend forty-five minutes learning more about any topic they choose while I circulate and answer questions. The last fifteen minutes are reserved for sharing and clarifying learning goals for home study.

I wrote the course and gladly share it. Feel free to use it in any way you wish. If you decide to model your own tarot class on my ideas, I only ask that you tell your students where you found it. Thank you for your interest in my work!

Workshop One: Getting Acquainted
MINI-LESSON: (50 MINUTES)

Introductions

Class expectations: What do you hope to learn? (Used to check in as a class again in Workshop 5.)

Brief history of tarot: Emphasizing the controversy of its history. (Who knows?)

So many choices: Types of decks and how to choose one right for you. (I bring a suitcase full of tarot decks to the first class, and lay them out on a table for people to look at on break and during the practice time.)

Getting acquainted with the cards: Ways to play with the cards, explaining the overall structure. (I also briefly mention its similarity to other esoteric systems, like astrology or the Tree of Life.)

Tarot journal

Rituals and tarot: Deciding what you value.

Bibliography/suggested reading (including great tarot websites)

BREAK: (10 MINUTES)

PRACTICE TIME: (45 MINUTES)

You might use this time for an explanation of creativity exercises using the tarot cards. I base this on my book *Tarot for the Healing Heart*, pages 96–98 (Llewellyn, 2001). You'll find suggestions for ways to play with the tarot that enhance intuition. A sampling of my ideas follows Workshop 6. (Or insert your own tarot "homework" here. This time is best used when students work on their own learning goals from the mini-lesson.)

REFLECTIONS: (15 MINUTES OF SHARING)

Workshop Two: The Minor Arcana
MINI-LESSON: (50 MINUTES)

Suits of the tarot: Wands, Cups, Swords, Pentacles (also mentioning the different names assigned suits like Staves and Rods).

The meaning of the tarot's numbers 1–10

Reducing numbers (example, 18 is a 9; 1 + 8 = 9)

Putting the suits and numbers together for general descriptions of the minor arcana cards

Reversed cards: Where to find the information, not how to read reversed.

BREAK: (10 MINUTES)

PRACTICE TIME/REFLECTIONS: (1 HOUR)

Workshop Three: The People of the Tarot
MINI-LESSON: (50 MINUTES)

The court cards: Pages, Knights, Queens, Kings (and other names assigned to them).

The court cards as an expression of their suits

The court cards: Other people or you? How to tell the difference.

Astrological associations of the court cards (optional)

BREAK: (10 MINUTES)

PRACTICE TIME/REFLECTIONS: (1 HOUR)

Workshop Four: The Fool's Journey
Mini-Lesson: (50 minutes)

The major arcana: The Fool through the World (Cards 0–21).

The 8–11 controversy

Astrological associations of the major arcana cards (optional)

Developing a worksheet with your own "catch phrases" for each major arcana card

Daily readings and the three-card spread

Break: (10 minutes)

Practice Time: (45 minutes)

Begin daily readings, reading for friends, family, and each other.

Reflections: (15 minutes)

Workshop Five: The Reading Process
Mini-Lesson: (50 minutes)

Checking in as a class: Do the goals of the class need to be changed at this time to reflect the needs of the class? (A teacher must be flexible. It is vital to reassess student expectations from Workshop 1 and adjust the teaching to reflect those needs. If students are not getting what they need from the teacher, now is the time to find out, not when an angry student demands a refund at the last class!)

Ethics and confidentiality

Designing your own layout (or introducing the Celtic Cross, or your favorite layout)

How to ask the right question before a reading

Building good narrative

Closure of a reading

Break: (10 minutes)

Practice Time/Reflections: (1 hour)

Workshop Six: Every Ending Is but a Beginning

No Mini-Lesson; entire class is interactive, with one break.

Because of time limitations, only two or three topics can realistically be discussed. It's up to the class or teacher to decide based on either a class vote or the personality of the class. Possible options include:

- Reading for each other

- Exchanging phone numbers

- Discussing ways to grow with tarot and how each person plans to use the tarot

- Tarot in cyberspace (tarot and computers, tarot software, websites to visit)

- Sharing types of layouts for specific situations

- Tips on becoming a professional reader (setting fees, advertising, business cards, finding a location to read, what to do with the angry or troubled seeker, when to issue refunds)

- Evaluation of the course: Did the course live up to your expectations? (This is invaluable feedback for the teacher: what worked, what didn't.)

- Sampling of creativity exercises designed to nurture intuition:

  1. Decorate your journal. Make it an expression of you.

  2. Think of people in the news. What court cards are they? For example, who is the U.S. president?

  3. Write your life story using only tarot card figures. Who are you? Who is your family?

  4. Write a story, compose a song, draw a picture, or pen a poem about one of the tarot cards that attracts you. Do the same with a card you dislike.

5. Create a tarot ritual that is meaningful for you. If rituals do not attract you, make an entry about that in your journal.

6. Make a journal entry about the relationship between your dreams and the tarot cards.

Advanced and Specialty Tarot Courses

In chapter 2, you learned that the law of supply and demand is a careful blending of your need to express your true self with your customer's need to have access to your skill, expertise, creative talents, and abilities. To create interest and expand your customer base, why not offer specialty or advanced tarot classes?

After you teach a beginning tarot course, advertise an advanced or specialized class. It can be open to all, but you can give discounts to the students who took your beginning class. Be sure to include "Basic knowledge of tarot required" in your ad.

For advanced topics in tarot, consider emphasizing one aspect of the tarot such as the court cards, the minor arcana, the major arcana, creating layouts, reading techniques, going pro with tarot, conducting phone readings, or the art of tarot reversals (read Mary K. Greer's *Complete Book of Tarot Reversals* first! [Llewellyn, 2002]).

While we're on the topic of using tarot books to teach, remember to honor copyright law because plagiarism is literary theft. If you plan to photocopy from the work of another, you must get written permission from the publisher and author to do so. Even if you don't photocopy, but use someone else's work or ideas, it is your literary responsibility to tell your class where you found the information and who the author is.

It is much less complicated to do what I do: I have my class buy the book! In this example, each student in my beginning class is required to buy Mary K. Greer's *Tarot for Your Self*. There are many wonderful tarot books on the market. What book will you use—or will you? Start thinking about that today because it takes time to get written permission from a publisher.

What will you include in your specialty classes? That depends on your interests and skill level. Look back in chapter 1 under the heading "The Myth of Competition." Here are some ideas for specialty classes: tarot and . . . aromatherapy, astrology, feng shui, herbs, spell work, financial planning, companion animal communication, ritual, storytelling, past-life regressions or karma, vocational or spiritual counseling, relationships, healing, business planning, or tarot as art.

What about tarot and shadow work? As author of *Tarot Shadow Work*, I advise you to be careful with this one. Because shadow work involves coming to terms with some of the most intimate aspects of life (and embarrassing or painful memories), I have not yet offered a shadow workshop. To me, a shadow workshop is akin to having therapy with the therapist's door wide open for all to hear the intimate details of one's life. It is slow, painful work and when repressed memories surface, professional help is often indicated. I don't feel that a short, casual group setting with strangers is appropriate for anything more than an introduction to what shadow work is, because shadow work cannot—and should not—be rushed or taken lightly.

The following is an example of a specialty tarot class using my book *Tarot for All Seasons*. I call it "Celebrating the Days and Nights of Power with Tarot." The focus of the course is to incorporate tarot into the eight holidays on the Wheel of the Year. There are several ways you could organize it depending on the needs of your community and the time you have available:

1. Offer a ten-week, pay-as-you-go course, with the first class serving as an introduction and the last class for ritual. The eight points on the Wheel are covered in the eight classes in between.

2. Offer a two-week class, one for introductory material and assignments and the second for sharing of student work and questions.

3. Conduct classes throughout the year and have the class times correspond to the points on the Wheel. In this method, you

advertise before each holiday and have two classes per holiday—one for background and assignments and one for sharing the students' holiday work.

In the example below, you'll find a ten-week course broken down into class-size parts based on *Tarot for All Seasons*. Where you start the Wheel depends on what time of year it is and your preference. For simplicity, I begin with Samhain. At the end of the section, I include a handout called "Creating Tarot Layouts the Easy Way." Feel free to photocopy it for use in your class. I ask only that you credit the method to me and tell your students where you found it.[1]

Workshop One: Getting Started

Introductions
An overview of the Wheel of the Year
Creating sacred space
Ritual and tarot
How to create a tarot layout (See handout at the end of appendix B)
Break
Students create tarot spreads based on the handout
Time for assignments, questions, and sharing of tarot spreads

Workshop Two: Samhain, October 31 (Halloween)

Questions from last workshop
Background, history, and description of Samhain
Discussion of appropriate magical workings for Samhain
Traditional Samhain ritual correspondences, including tarot cards, scents, magical brews, and candles
Break
Either have students do the Fruit of Wisdom layout on pages 54–55 of *Tarot for All Seasons* or have them create their own Samhain layout using the method taught in the first class.[2]
Sharing of Samhain layouts/rituals and questions

Workshop Three: Yule, circa December 21 or 22
(Winter Solstice)

Questions from last workshop

Description of Yule

Discussion of appropriate magical workings for Yule

Traditional Yule ritual correspondences, including tarot cards, scents, magical brews, and candles

Break

Either have students do the Solstice Light layout on pages 61–63 of *Tarot for All Seasons* or have them create their own Yule layout using the method taught in the first class.

Sharing of Yule layouts/rituals and questions

Workshop Four: Imbolc, February 2

Questions from last workshop

Description of Imbolc

Discussion of appropriate magical workings for Imbolc

Traditional Imbolc ritual correspondences, including tarot cards, scents, magical brews, and candles

Break

Either have students do the Brid's Wheel layout on pages 69–71 of *Tarot for All Seasons* or have them create their own Imbolc layout using the method taught in the first class.

Sharing of Imbolc layouts/rituals and questions

Workshop Five: Ostara, March 21
(Spring or Vernal Equinox)

Questions from last workshop

Description of Ostara

Discussion of appropriate magical workings for Ostara

Traditional Ostara ritual correspondences, including tarot cards, scents, magical brews, and candles

Break

Either have students do the Metamorphosis layout on pages 77–79 of
Tarot for All Seasons or have them create their own Ostara layout
using the method taught in the first class.

Sharing of Ostara layouts/rituals and questions

Workshop Six: Beltane, April 30 (May Eve)

Questions from last workshop

Description of Beltane

Discussion of appropriate magical workings for Beltane

Traditional Beltane ritual correspondences, including tarot cards,
scents, magical brews, and candles

Break

Either have students do the May Queen layout on pages 85–87 of
Tarot for All Seasons or have them create their own Beltane layout
using the method taught in the first class.

Sharing of Beltane layouts/rituals and questions

Workshop Seven: Midsummer, circa June 21 (Summer Solstice, Litha)

Questions from last workshop

Description of Midsummer

Discussion of appropriate magical workings for Midsummer

Traditional Midsummer ritual correspondences, including tarot cards,
scents, magical brews, and candles

Break

Either have students do the Midsummer's Dream layout on pages
92–94 of *Tarot for All Seasons* or have them create their own Midsummer layout using the method taught in the first class.

Sharing of Midsummer layouts/rituals and questions

Workshop Eight: Lughnasadh, August 1 (Lammas)

Questions from last workshop

Description of Lughnasadh

Discussion of appropriate magical workings for Lughnasadh

Traditional Lughnasadh ritual correspondences, including tarot cards, scents, magical brews, and candles

Break

Either have students do the Harvest Home layout on pages 101–104 of *Tarot for All Seasons* or have them create their own Lughnasadh layout using the method taught in the first class.

Sharing of Lughnasadh layouts/rituals and questions

Workshop Nine: Mabon, September 21 (Autumnal or Fall Equinox)

Questions from last workshop

Description of Mabon

Discussion of appropriate magical workings for Mabon

Traditional Mabon ritual correspondences, including tarot cards, scents, magical brews, and candles

Break

Either have students do the Balance of Power layout on pages 110–113 of *Tarot for All Seasons* or have them create their own Mabon layout using the method taught in the first class.

Sharing of Mabon layouts/rituals and questions

Workshop Ten: Every Ending Is but a Beginning

This is very open-ended depending on the needs of your class. Possibilities include:

- Discussing chapter 6 of *Tarot for All Seasons* called "A Year and a Day." It describes magical ways to study the tarot and use of tarot in magical spells.

- Discussing future plans of ways to learn with the tarot.

- Doing seasonal layouts for each other.

- Sharing seasonal tarot rituals and layouts.

- How about each student bringing a seasonal dish if you have also incorporated holiday food into your correspondences? Have a tarot potluck buffet and reading party.

- Will everyone dress as his or her favorite tarot card? Throw a tarot masquerade party.

- Insert your own wonderful activity here.

Of course, by now, you may have had a creative burst and decided to offer a specialty class based on your own spiritual traditions. Great, go for it—that's what learning and growing with the cards we love so much is all about. Have fun!

Creating Tarot Layouts the Easy Way

This serves as a guide to basic layout creation. With practice, more complicated spreads will evolve over time.

1. Decide upon a subject for your layout. Anything that is of concern to you such as finances, relationships, work/career, creativity, healing, spirituality, and so on.

2. Write at least a page about the subject without censoring any thoughts. Take at least five minutes to do this. If it's a subject you need to research, make a note of that too. For instance, in *Tarot for the Healing Heart*, I had to research the stages of grief before I could create a spread for it. To get you started:

   a. "I want to create a tarot spread on this subject because . . ."

   b. Answer questions about the subject: Who? What? Why? When? Where? How?

3. Underline words and phrases from your paragraphs that jump out at you. They become your positions. Note how many you have. Could any of them be condensed into one position?

4. Add the "layout plus one" card; either an advice/next step position or a future position.

5. Decide if the words or phrases are questions or statements, or a combination.

6. Place them in a logical sequence of thought. The positions should flow one from the other. What is first? What is second? and so on. You will find that they often place themselves. Or does it matter which is first and second, etc.? Sometimes it doesn't.

7. Decide upon a shape for the layout that symbolically represents the subject of your spread. For example, a layout about a new love could be in the shape of Cupid's arrow. Finances could be in the shape of a dollar sign. Is it linear or circular? When I'm in doubt, I tend to create rows.

8. Place your position topics from numbers 3 and 4 into the chosen shape. Look at it and sense the flow. Do the questions tell a story? If it doesn't flow, rearrange the positions in your chosen shape until it does flow, or at least makes sense going from one to the other. If you use rows, look for any horizontal or perpendicular relationships to the positions. Does reading up and down or across add anything?

9. Never hesitate to change, add, or delete, but stay with the chosen layout during the actual reading to pinpoint kinks and see where it doesn't flow. Take notes. Write an entry in your journal about why it did or didn't work. Make changes until you are satisfied.

10. Have a friend do the layout and get feedback. (optional)

Time frame: About one hour

The goal isn't to create a perfect layout in one hour, but to learn a process that you can develop over time.

15 minutes: An overview of the method.

5 minutes: Everyone chooses a topic as individuals and writes a page about it.

10 minutes: Underline keywords and pull them out of the written page. Number them. Add "layout plus one" (Advice/Next Step or Future).

10 minutes: Think of a symbolic shape and place the positions into that shape.

20 minutes: Sharing of new layouts or a time for questions.

© 2003 by Christine Jette

Appendix C ‖ The Resourceful Reader

Not all who wander are lost.

— J. R. R. Tolkien

Learn as much as possible about small business before starting your
tarot consultation service. Careful preliminary planning will contribute to the success of your venture. This book takes a "hands-on"
approach to professional tarot card reading, but don't limit yourself to
one book. I'd like to think it's a great place to start, but you have many
resources available to you.

Branch out and learn more through books, workshops, and online
research. The library holds a wealth of information for the entrepre-
neur. Don't overlook your local Chamber of Commerce and other
professional readers for advice. Tarot organizations and small business
associations provide an opportunity to network. Why struggle alone
when other people in the same industry share so many of your concerns? Local technical or community colleges and universities often
carry inexpensive noncredit business courses through the continuing
education department.

The following recommendations include business, psychology, and
tarot resources, online and off. They serve only as a launching place
for your personal exploration. I have listed them because I've found
them useful, but that doesn't mean I have the final word on anything.

You will find that each resource also carries its own links or recommended reading list. The possibilities to learn more are endless. Consider, too, that the web is constantly changing. All the information in this appendix was accurate at the time of publication.

Business Books

Start by reviewing the bibliography. I found all business books listed to be very helpful. I won't buy a book unless it's user-friendly. I especially recommend:

Adams, Bob. *Small Business Start-Up: Your Comprehensive Guide to Starting and Managing a Business*. Holbrook, Mass.: Adams Media Corporation, 1996.

Bailey, Maria T. *The Women's Home-Based Business Book of Answers*. Roseville, Calif.: Prima Publishing, Random House, 2001.

Bridges, Carol. *The Medicine Woman's Guide to Being in Business for Yourself*. Nashville, Ind.: Earth Nation Publishing, 1992.

Jessup, Claudia, and Genie Chipps. *A Woman's Guide to Starting a Business*. New York: Henry Holt and Company, 1991.

Levinson, Jay Conrad. *Guerrilla Marketing: Secrets for Making Big Profits from Your Small Business*. New York: Houghton-Mifflin, 1998.

Milano, Carol. *HERS: The Wise Woman's Guide to Starting a Business on $2000 or Less*. New York: Allworth Press, 1991.

Sohnen-Moe, Cherie. *Business Mastery: A Guide for Creating a Fulfilling, Thriving Business and Keeping It Successful*. 3d ed. Tucson, Ariz.: Sohnen-Moe Associates, Inc., 1988.

Business Organizations

Also see the "Business and Finance" section under "On the Web" below. Sites carry many links for all types of business organizations.

Hint: There were 435 entries when I typed "small business organizations" in the Yahoo.com search box. It included everything from the American Association of Black Women Entrepreneurs to the National Association for the Self-Employed. I'll list the main one to get you started.

United States Small Business Administration
1111 Eighteenth Street NW, Sixth Floor
Washington, D.C. 20036
(202) 606-4000
Toll-free hotline: (800) 368-5855
www.sbaonline.sba.gov

Books/Magazines for Starting and Maintaining an Online Business

Holden, Greg. *Starting an Online Business Book for Dummies*. Foster City, Calif.: IDG Books Worldwide, 2000.

Kobler, Ronald D., et al, eds. *Smart Computing Learning Series: Web Tools*. Lincoln, Nebr.: Sandhills Publishing Company, 2002. (This is a magazine that can be purchased at almost any bookstore or large magazine rack. I buy mine at a grocery store.)

Liflander, Rob. *The Everything Online Business Book: Use the Internet to Build Your Business*. Holbrook, Mass.: Adams Media Corporation, 2000.

The Counseling Process

Not one of the following four books uses the word *tarot* or discusses professional tarot reading. However, all four contain a treasure-house of wisdom about the counseling process that is immediately applicable to reading the cards.

Cunningham, Donna. *The Consulting Astrologer's Guidebook*. York Beach, Maine: Samuel Weiser, Inc., 1994. (The whole book is wonderful. Simply substitute the words *tarot* or *reading* for the words *astrology* or *chart* and everything applies to the professional tarot reader.)

Kennedy, Eugene, and Sara C. Charles, M.D. *On Becoming a Counselor: A Basic Guide for Nonprofessional Counselors and Other Helpers*. 3d ed. New York: Crossroad Publishing Company, 2001. (Answers the one important question: What can we really do to help another?)

Lauver, Phillip, and David R. Harvey. *The Practical Counselor: Elements of Effective Helping*. Pacific Grove, Calif.: Brooks/Cole Publishing Co., 1997. (Warm, compassionate textbook about the process of counseling.)

Marks, Tracy. *The Art of Chart Interpretation*. Sebastopol, Calif.: CRS Publications, 1986. (Especially part three: "The Process of Astrological Counseling.")

On the Web

Business and Finance

Idea Café
www.ideacafe.com

Information, quizzes, and resources for small-business owners with a light, humorous touch. With handy tips and message board.

Service Core of Retired Executives
www.score.org

Information and advice from seasoned business people. You can locate the chapter nearest you. Counseling is free of charge.

Business Nation
www.businessnation.com

Small-business and start-up information, resources, articles, search engines, franchise opportunities, auctions, barters, expert advice, news, discussion forums.

Internal Revenue Service
www.irs.gov

Believe it or not, this site is updated and user-friendly. Carries a lot of information for the small-business person. From the home page, click "Business" and then "Small Business."

E-mail Advertising
www.findmorebuyers.com/page.cfm/198

Excellent free advice on how to write e-mail ads.

Psychology/Psychiatry/Counseling/Health

American Psychiatric Association
www.psych.org/public_info/index.cfm

American Psychological Association
http://helping.apa.org

Both sites carry a wealth of useful information that can be applied to the counseling aspect of professional tarot reading. Everything from coping with the threat of terrorism, post-traumatic stress disorder, grief, and substance abuse to burnout.

Health A to Z
www.healthatoz.com

Start your health search here. This comprehensive site has information on both traditional health care and alternative/complementary therapies. Many links.

Search Engines

Find everything you're looking for by using powerful search engines. My favorites are

www.go.com (formerly www.infoseek.com)
www.yahoo.com
www.lycos.com
www.altavista.com

Getting Rid of Unwanted Junk E-mail (Spam)

www.cauce.org

The Coalition Against Unsolicited Commercial E-mail carries great tips on how to rid your in-box of junk. I have cut my Spam encounters by two-thirds.

Tarot

Please note: Computer terminology can be confusing. E-lists, message boards, and chat rooms are not the same. With e-lists, discussion takes place through e-mail. You can find a list for just about everything including the tarot. Some tarot e-lists are moderated while some are not. I prefer moderated lists because you can receive a lot of unrelated postings and flamers abound when there is no moderator.

E-lists can consume huge amounts of time. One option is to select "Digest" and receive only ten to twenty e-mails at a time instead of the whole lot. The other option is to "Read E-mails Online"—you don't get any e-mail correspondence, but you can check into the server and read what has been written that day.

Chat rooms involve people chatting online in real time and they are interactive. In other words, you are all online at the same time and communicating with one another in the moment. Message boards are usually found at a website. You can post messages for all to see and respond to other messages. No e-mail is involved. You post your message through the server and it stays at the server site. The host usually reserves the right to delete inappropriate messages and can block flamers from the site.

E-lists, message boards, and chat rooms can be addictive and eat the clock. There is no guarantee of quality and some of the communication is downright nasty. Something changes people when they are anonymous in front of a computer screen. I'll never understand the wisdom of arguing online with strangers I'll never meet, but that's just me. Tarot e-lists, message boards, and chat rooms are worth a try because they can be fun, informative, and a great way to locate like-minded souls. Search until you find something that fits your style and personality.

Tarot E-Lists

www.yahoogroups.com

When I typed "tarot" in the search box, I received 857 entries! Try All Things Tarot for professional tarot readers at: http://groups.yahoo.com/group/AllThingsTarot.

The two best are not listed. I suggest you go to www.tarotpassages.com and click "Links" on the home page. There you will find:

TarotL@egroups.com: www.lightspeed.bc.ca/hilander/tarot.html

Comparative Tarot: www.egroups.com/group/ComparativeTarot

Tarot Chat Rooms

www.msn.com

From the home page, click "People and Chat." Type "tarot" in the search box. I found 516 entries.

Message Boards

Salem Tarot Page: www.salemtarot.com/core.html

From the home page, click "Journal." This message board is more about the Craft than tarot, but tarot comments do pop up. Well moderated. Flamers are blocked from future entries and respect for differences is encouraged. You can also send a free tarot postcard to a friend. Many resources and links to things not quite tarot. Located in Salem, Massachusetts, this site is . . . bewitching.

Free Tarot Readings on the Web

Llewellyn's Free Web Readings
www.webtarot.net

Fun with a good choice of decks and layouts. Can also be located by clicking "Tarot Readings" from Llewellyn's home page:

www.llewellyn.com

Façade
www.facade.com

The most thorough free reading I found.

Free Reading Network
www.freereading.net

Free reading with a real person, sponsored by the American Tarot Association.

Tarot.com
www.tarot.com/reading/select.php

Very short readings.

Tarot Organizations

American Tarot Association
1910 Thatcher Boulevard, #205
Safford, Arizona 85546
Phone: 800-372-1524
Website: www.ata-tarot.com

International Tarot Society
P.O. Box 1475
Morton Grove, Illinois 60053
Phone: 847-965-9916
Website: www.tarotsociety.org

Tarot Websites

Tarot Passages with Diane Wilkes
www.tarotpassages.com

I believe Tarot Passages is the best tarot site on the web today with regular updates and many links. A wonderful resource. Bookmark and enjoy.

Tarot Insights with Nellie Levine
www.illuminationtarot.com/insights/index.html

If this site hasn't won an award, it should. Ms. Levine offers tips for beginners, tarot links, and her question-and-answer section is well done. With reviews, articles, a recommended book list, and updates.

Tarot Moon with Thrysse
www.tarotmoon.com/tarotmoon.html

Thrysse carries a thorough tarot FAQ section. Her article on formulating your question helps you get the most out of a reading. A well-organized and beautiful site.

Future Insights with Linda Corteselli
www.futureinsights.net/index.html

Ms. Corteselli is a professional astrologer and tarot reader. She is the author and artist of a nontraditional sixty-card tarot deck called *Nature Speaks* based on the natural world. Her FAQ sections for both tarot and astrology are thorough. A great place to begin your journey.

Moon Arcana
www.moonarcana.com

Moon Arcana offers something for everyone with good tarot information and links. You can "walk through the garden, gaze at the stars, shop for treasures, surf the web of shadows or browse for books." Enchanting graphics.

Rebel Planet Magazine with book reviewer Devon Cathlin
www.lunarace.com/planet.html

A one-stop site for all things esoteric, including the tarot. Carries an extensive tarot deck and book review section accessed from the home page. Winner of the Tarot Ace Award.

Aeclectic Tarot
www.aeclectic.net/tarot/index.html

There is something for everyone at this site. View cards from over 350 decks, or read tarot book and software reviews. All reviews carry star ratings ranging from wonderful (five stars) to don't bother (one star). Books and software sold in partnership with Amazon.com. Also has an information section for beginners and a tarot discussion forum. Enjoy a free reading via Tarot.com. With links and regular updates.

Finding the Muse with Christine Jette
www.findingthemuse.com

Yep, this is my own little website. It covers an array of topics including astrology, the Age of Aquarius, tarot, shadow work, creativity, music, poetry, the sacred feminine, and healing, to the heady joys and profound frustrations of writing—with a feline or two on the Catnip page. Feature articles change monthly as the Sun Sign changes and I post interesting links as I find them. So, come discover the stars as you explore the one-and-only you in tarot . . .

Tarot Books and Decks

This is a trick section because I can't decide what is best for you. I am hesitant to give advice about books and decks. We each must find our own way in the world of tarot. The best that I can do is share what has worked for me. I urge you to search until you find books and decks that resonate within you. You will know when you have found them. Something inside you will say, "Yes, this is it."

I love any tarot book written by Mary K. Greer or Rachel Pollack. Try Greer's *Tarot for Your Self*. It is a book of self-transformation written in a user-friendly workbook format. Her major contribution, in my opinion, is offering a way to learn the cards without parroting someone else's definitions by rote memorization. Mary K. Greer was the first author to bring the cards to life and make them real in everyday living for me.

I believe Rachel Pollack's *Seventy-Eight Degrees of Wisdom: A Book of Tarot* stands as the all-time definitive work on the subject. I love Pollack's work because of her use of myth and psychology in working with the cards.

There are over one hundred tarot decks on the market today. With so many choices, how do you decide? Again, select decks that appeal to you. If you simply can't choose, start with the *Rider Tarot* deck published by U.S. Games. Designed in the early twentieth century by Pamela Coleman Smith under the direction of Arthur Edward Waite, it is considered to be the prototype of all decks to follow.

Sometimes called the *Waite Tarot* or the *Rider-Waite Tarot,* the outstanding feature is that all of the cards have divinatory pictures on them. Up until that time, the forty pip cards (numeral cards one to ten in each of the four suits) depicted only their correct number of Wands, Cups, Swords, and Pentacles. In other words, the Three of Cups showed three cups, not three dancing ladies, and so on.

Choose a deck based on your personal tastes, philosophy, and frame of reference. For example, I love the *Robin Wood Tarot* deck published by Llewellyn. It's so pretty. But since I am a Libra Sun, Libra Rising

(Cancer Moon), of course I want things to be pretty! The truth is, the *Robin Wood* deck is much too pretty (and caucasian) for some people. No two decks are the same. Some are traditional, that is, based on the Rider model, while others take a more diverse course. Shop around and play with a lot of tarot decks. You will know when you find the one, or twelve, right for you. Enjoy the journey.

Notes

Chapter 1

1. David H. Bangs, *The Start Up Guide: A One-Year Plan for Entrepreneurs* (Chicago: Upstart Publishing, 1994), 3–4.
2. Maria Nemeth, *The Energy of Money: A Spiritual Guide to Financial and Personal Fulfillment* (New York: Ballantine Publishing Group, 1997), 39.
3. Christine Jette, *Tarot for the Healing Heart* (St. Paul, Minn.: Llewellyn Publications, 2001), 117–18.
4. Susan Jane Gilman, *Kiss My Tiara: How to Rule the World As a Smart-mouth Goddess* (New York: Warner Books, 2001), 144.
5. Donna Cunningham, *The Consulting Astrologer's Guidebook* (York Beach, Maine: Samuel Weiser, Inc., 1994), 199.
6. Nemeth, *The Energy of Money,* 287.

Chapter 2

1. Marcia Stanhope and Jeanette Lancaster, "Tips for the Home Visit," in *Community Health Nursing,* 2d ed. (Boston: Mosby-Year Book, Inc., 1996), 49–50.
2. Carol Bridges, *The Medicine Woman's Guide to Being in Business for Yourself* (Nashville, Ind.: Earth Nation Publishing, 1992), 15.
3. David H. Bangs, *The Start Up Guide: A One-Year Plan for Entrepreneurs* (Chicago: Upstart Publishing, 1994), 87–90.
4. Claudia Jessup and Genie Chipps, *A Woman's Guide to Starting a Business* (New York: Henry Holt and Company, 1991), 47–48.

5. Ibid., 83–84.

6. Robert W. Bly, *The Copywriter's Handbook: A Step-by-Step Guide to Writing Copy that Sells* (New York: Henry Holt and Co., 1990), 115.

7. Bob Adams, *Small Business Start-Up: Your Comprehensive Guide to Starting and Managing a Business* (Holbrook, Mass.: Adams Media Corp., 1996), 207.

8. Joelle Steele, *How to Market Your Astrological Services* (Pacific Grove, Calif.: Park Place Publications, 1998), 15.

9. Lori Mangold and Scott Mangold, *The Professional Pet Sitter: A Guide to Starting and Operating A Successful Service* (Portland, Ore.: Paws-itive Press, 1995), 39.

10. Patti J. Moran, *Pet Sitting for Profit: A Complete Manual for Professional Success* (New York: Howell Book House, 1997), 153–55.

Chapter 3

1. Rob Liflander, *The Everything Online Business Book: Use the Internet to Build Your Business* (Holbrook, Mass.: Adams Media Corporation, 2000), 54.

2. Gregory Anderson, "Looks Aren't Everything, But . . . Keep Design Issues in Mind When Building Your Site," *Smart Computing Learning Series: Web Tools*, vol. 8, issue 1 (Lincoln, Nebr.: Sandhills Publishing Company, 2002), 12.

3. Greg Holden, *Starting an Online Business Book for Dummies* (Foster City, Calif.: IDG Books Worldwide, 2000), 335.

4. Liflander, *The Everything Online Business Book,* 116.

5. Coalition Against Unsolicited Commercial E-mail, 2002, www.cauce.org.

6. "Terms of Agreement," 2002, http://www.liszt.com/pop/index.html?mode=terms.

7. Cherie M. Sohnen-Moe, *Business Mastery* (Tucson, Ariz.: Sohnen-Moe Associates, Inc., 1997), 161.

8. PNC Bank, Cincinnati, Ohio, Merchant Credit Card Account. Information obtained by author during interview with customer service representative, 2002.

9. Ibid.

10. Cincinnati Bell, "Sales Tips: Selling Over the Telephone," Cincinnati, Ohio, 2002.

11. Harold I. Kaplan, M.D. and Benjamin J. Sadock, M.D., "Psychiatric Emergencies," in *Synopsis of Psychiatry*, 6th ed. (Baltimore, Md.: Williams and Wilkins, 1991), 151 and 160.
12. Ibid., 556.
13. Federal Trade Commission, Children's Online Privacy Protection Act (COPPA), 1998, www.ftc.gov/ogc/coppa1.htm.
14. Finding the Muse, home page of Christine Jette, 2002, www.findingthemuse.com/index.html.
15. The text of this e-mail is copyrighted by Diane Wilkes and is used here by permission of Diane Wilkes.

Chapter 4

1. Maria T. Bailey, *The Women's Home-Based Business Book of Answers* (Roseville, Calif.: Prima Publishing, Random House, 2001), 144–45.
2. Lori Mangold and Scott Mangold, *The Professional Pet Sitter: A Guide to Starting and Operating A Successful Service* (Portland, Ore.: Paws-itive Press, 1995), 11–12.
3. Carol Milano, *HERS: The Wise Woman's Guide to Starting a Business on $2000 or Less* (New York: Allworth Press, 1991), 133.
4. Cheryle Jones Syracuse and William Owen, *Ohio State University Fact Sheet* (Columbus, Ohio: Office of Community Development, 2002), http://ohioline.osu.edu/cd-fact/1201.html.
5. Greater Cincinnati Chamber of Commerce (Cincinnati, Ohio, 2002), www.gccc.com/home.htm.
6. Syracuse and Owen, *Ohio State University Fact Sheet.*
7. Cathy Mong, "Fortune Telling Faces Shadowy Future," *Dayton Daily News*, January 25, 2001. www.daytondailynews.com.
8. Ibid.
9. Cathy Mong, "Moraine's Seer Ban Panned," *Dayton Daily News*, January 26, 2001. www.daytondailynews.com.
10. Ibid.
11. Brad Bunnin and Peter Beren, *The Writer's Legal Companion* (Reading, Mass.: Perseus Books, 1998), 203.
12. Tad Crawford, *The Writer's Legal Guide* (New York: Allworth Press, 1998), 233.
13. IRS Public Information, http://www.irs.gov/business/small/display/0,,i1=2&i2=23&genericId=20852,00.html.

14. IRS Public Information,
    http://www.irs.gov/business/small/display/0,,i1=2&i2=
    23&genericId=20850,00.html.
15. Patti J. Moran, *Pet Sitting for Profit: A Complete Manual for Professional Success* (New York: Howell Book House, 1997), 70.
16. Note: Computers have quartz crystal in their internal workings. To attune myself to the energy of the computer, I keep several crystals on and around it, especially near the modem. I need all the help I can get.
17. Cherie M. Sohnen-Moe, *Business Mastery* (Tucson, Ariz.: Sohnen-Moe Associates, Inc., 1997), 190.
18. Bob Adams, *Small Business Start-Up: Your Comprehensive Guide to Starting and Managing a Business* (Holbrook, Mass.: Adams Media Corporation, 1996), 61.

Chapter 5

1. Barbara Ann Brennan, *Light Emerging: The Journey of Personal Healing* (New York: Bantam Books, 1993), 161.
2. Please note: Another way to describe the negative contract is to call it a part of the personal shadow. My first book, *Tarot Shadow Work*, addresses breaking through the pain that keeps us in limited, unhealthy relationships.
3. Cynthia Giles, *The Tarot: Methods, Mastery and More* (New York: Simon and Schuster, 1996), 164.
4. Ibid., 8.
5. Thomas L. Clayton, M.D., ed., *Taber's Cyclopedic Medical Dictionary* (Philadelphia, Pa.: F.A. Davis Company, 1993), 410.
6. Donna Cunningham, *The Consulting Astrologer's Guidebook* (York Beach, Maine: Samuel Weiser, Inc., 1994), 55.
7. Kenneth N. Anderson and Lois E. Anderson, eds., *Mosby's Pocket Dictionary of Medicine, Nursing and Allied Health* (St. Louis, Mo.: CV Mosby Company, 1990), 360.
8. Clayton, *Taber's Cyclopedic Medical Dictionary*, 943.
9. Eugene Kennedy and Sara C. Charles, M.D., *On Becoming a Counselor: A Basic Guide for Nonprofessional Counselors and Other Helpers*, 3d ed. (New York: Crossroad Publishing Company, 2001), 150.
10. Phillip Lauver and David R. Harvey, *The Practical Counselor: Elements of Effective Helping* (Pacific Grove, Calif.: Brooks/Cole Publishing Co., 1997), 227.

11. Ibid.
12. Christine Jette, *Tarot for the Healing Heart* (St. Paul, Minn.: Llewellyn Publications, 2001), 106.
13. Kennedy and Charles, *On Becoming a Counselor,* 112.
14. Arthur S. Reber, *The Penguin Dictionary of Psychology* (New York: Penguin Books, 1985), 364.
15. Ibid., 296.
16. I am in no way discounting the problems of teen boys. They, too, live in an impossible world of cultural media myths. Males are bombarded every day with mixed messages of masculinity. For an in-depth yet compassionate look at violence among teenage boys, I recommend *Lost Boys: Why Our Sons Are Violent and How We Can Save Them* by James Gabardino, Ph.D. (Free Press, 1999). To learn more about male wounding, I suggest *Under Saturn's Shadow: The Wounding and Healing of Men* by James Hollis (Book World, 1994) or try David Tracy's *Remaking Men: Jung Spirituality and Social Change* (Routledge, 1997).

    The information here, covering methods of communication with teens, is valid regardless of gender. I have chosen to address the specific cultural myths of girls because I am most familiar with them. When reading for teen males, please use your own life experience and sensitivity and adjust your readings accordingly.
17. Janet Clausen and Marilyn Kielbasa, "Of Myths and Mermaids: Nurturing the Spirituality of Adolescent Girls," *America Magazine*, September 24, 2001: 21.
18. Ibid., 20.
19. Melvin Lewis, M.D. and Fred R. Volkmar, M.D., *Clinical Aspects of Child and Adolescent Development* (Philadelphia: Lea and Febiger, 1990), 219.
20. Ibid., 218.
21. Anthony Storr, *The Art of Psychotherapy* (New York: Routledge, Chapman and Hall, Inc., 1989), 15.
22. William C. Burton, *Burton's Legal Thesaurus*, 3d ed. (New York: McGraw-Hill, 1998), 159.

Chapter 6

1. Gary R. Muschla, *Writing Workshop Survival Kit* (New York: Center for Applied Research in Education, 1993), 8.
2. Ibid., 3.

3. So that my workshops don't produce profound sleepiness, I allow for many breaks. The mind is easily put on information overload. Workshops are sedentary and blood pools in the feet. Physical activity restores blood flow to the brain and enhances learning.

   Offer fruit juices and whole grain snacks, not drinks made with refined sugar or pastries with only fat calories. Unsweetened juice and complex carbohydrates are fine sources of energy. Heavily sweetened drinks and pastries made with white sugar cause the blood sugar to plummet in about two hours due to an overproduction of insulin. Fatty foods, such as pastries and chips, cause the majority of the blood flow to enter the digestive system, resulting in sleepiness.
4. Caroline Green, ed., *Mosby's Conventional Medicine/Alternative Medicine: Choices of Treatment for Your Most Common Medical Problems* (St. Louis, Mo.: Mosby Year Books, Inc, 1998), 98.
5. Stephanie Judy, *Making Music for the Joy of It* (Los Angeles, Calif.: Jeremy P. Tarcher, Inc., 1990), 261–62.
6. Harold I. Kaplan, M.D. and Benjamin J. Sadock, M.D., *Pocket Handbook of Clinical Psychiatry*, 6th ed. (Baltimore, Md.: Williams and Wilkins, 1990), 165.
7. Judy, *Making Music*, 65.

Epilogue

1. American Psychological Association, "Psychology at Work: The Road to Burnout," the APA Help Center: Get the Facts, online public information, http://helping.apa.org/work/stress6.html.
2. Ibid.
3. American Psychological Association, "Psychology in Daily Life: Stress," the APA Help Center: Get the Facts, online public information, http://helping.apa.org/daily/naps.html.
4. Caroline Green, ed., *Mosby's Conventional Medicine/Alternative Medicine: Choices of Treatment for Your Most Common Medical Problems* (St. Louis, Mo.: Mosby Year Books, Inc, 1998), 90.

Appendix A

1. Ms. Wilkes is also a professional astrologer with over twenty years of experience.

2. "Diane Wilkes's Tarot Code of Ethics" is copyrighted by Diane Wilkes and is used here by permission of Diane Wilkes.

Appendix B

1. "Creating Tarot Layouts the Easy Way" has been marked with a copyright symbol (©). If reproducing this material, do not remove this symbol.
2. I believe each student creating his or her own layout is always best.

Bibliography

Adams, Bob. *Small Business Start-Up: Your Comprehensive Guide to Starting and Managing a Business.* Holbrook, Mass.: Adams Media Corporation, 1996.

American Psychological Association. "Psychology in Daily Life—Stress: How and When to Get Help," www.apa.org (http://helping.apa.org/daily/naps.html), 2001.

———. "Psychology at Work: The Road to Burnout," www.apa.org (http://helping.apa.org/work/stress6.html), 2001.

Anderson, Gregory. "Looks Aren't Everything, But . . . Keep Design Issues in Mind When Building Your Site." *Smart Computing* 8, no. 1 (2002): 11–15.

Anderson, Kenneth N., and Lois E. Anderson, eds. *Mosby's Pocket Dictionary of Medicine, Nursing and Allied Health.* St. Louis, Mo.: CV Mosby Co., 1990.

Arroyo, Stephen. M.A. *Astrology, Psychology and the Four Elements: An Energy Approach to Astrology and Its Use in the Counseling Arts.* Sebastopol, Calif.: CRCS Publications, 1975.

Avery, Brice. *Thorson's Principles of Psychotherapy.* San Francisco: Harper-Collins Publishers, 1996.

Bailey, Maria T. *The Women's Home-Based Business Book of Answers.* Roseville, Calif.: Prima Publishing, Random House, 2001.

Bangs, David H. Jr. *The Start Up Guide: A One-Year Plan for Entrepreneurs.* Chicago: Upstart Publishing, 1994.

Benares, Camden. *Common Sense Tarot.* Van Nuys, Calif.: Newcastle Publishing Company, 1992.

Bly, Robert W. *The Copywriter's Handbook: A Step-by-Step Guide to Writing Copy That Sells.* New York: Henry Holt and Company, 1990.

————. *Secrets of a Freelance Writer.* New York: Henry Holt, 1998.

Brennan, Barbara Ann. *Light Emerging: The Journey of Personal Healing.* New York: Bantam Books, 1993.

Bridges, Carol. *The Medicine Woman's Guide to Being in Business for Yourself.* Nashville, Ind.: Earth Nation Publishing, 1992.

Bunnin, Brad, and Peter Beren. *The Writer's Legal Companion.* Reading, Mass.: Perseus Books, 1998.

Burton, William C. *Burton's Legal Thesaurus*, 3d ed. New York: McGraw-Hill, 1998.

Cameron, Julia. *The Artist's Way: A Spiritual Path to Higher Creativity.* New York: Penguin Putnam, 1992.

Clarson, Laura. *Tarot Unveiled: The Method to Its Magic.* Stamford, Conn.: U.S. Games Systems, Inc., 1988.

Clausen, Janet, and Marilyn Kielbasa. "Of Myths and Mermaids: Nurturing the Spirituality of Adolescent Girls." *America Magazine* (24 September 2001): 21.

Clayton, Thomas L., M.D., ed. *Taber's Cyclopedic Medical Dictionary.* Philadelphia, Pa.: F.A. Davis Company, 1993.

Coalition Against Unsolicited Commercial E-mail, www.cauce.org, 2002.

Cook, John. *The Book of Positive Quotations.* Minneapolis, Minn.: Fairview Press, 1993.

Crawford, Tad. *The Writer's Legal Guide.* New York: Allworth Press, 1998.

Cunningham, Donna. *The Consulting Astrologer's Guidebook.* York Beach, Maine: Samuel Weiser, Inc., 1994.

Dayton Daily News, www.daytondailynews.com, Dayton, Ohio, 2001.

Echols, Signe E., et al., *Spiritual Tarot: Seventy-Eight Paths to Personal Enlightenment*. New York: Avon Books, 1996.

Fairfield, Gail. *Choice Centered Tarot*. York Beach, Maine: Samuel Weiser, Inc., 1997.

Federal Trade Commission, www.ftc.gov, 2002.

Finding the Muse, www.findingthemuse.com, home page of Christine Jette, 2002.

Giles, Cynthia. *The Tarot: History, Mystery and Lore*. New York: Simon and Schuster, 1992.

———. *The Tarot: Methods, Mastery and More*. New York: Simon and Schuster, 1996.

Gilman, Susan Jane. *Kiss My Tiara: How to Rule the World As a Smartmouth Goddess*. New York: Warner Books, 2001.

Gordon, Richard. *The Intuitive Tarot*. Nevada City, Calif.: Blue Dolphin Publishing, Inc., 1994.

Green, Caroline, ed. *Mosby's Conventional Medicine/Alternative Medicine: Choices of Treatment for Your Most Common Medical Problems*. St. Louis, Mo.: Mosby Year Books, Inc, 1998.

Greer, Mary K. *The Complete Book of Tarot Reversals*. St. Paul, Minn.: Llewellyn Publications, 2002.

———. *Tarot Constellations*. North Hollywood, Calif.: Newcastle Publishing Co., 1987.

———. *Tarot for Your Self*. North Hollywood, Calif.: Newcastle Publishing Co., 1984.

———. *Tarot Mirrors*. North Hollywood, Calif.: Newcastle Publishing Co., 1988.

Hanmaker-Zondag, Karen. *Tarot as a Way of Life: A Jungian Approach to the Tarot*. York Beach, Maine: Samuel Weiser, Inc., 1994.

Holden, Greg. *Starting an Online Business Book for Dummies*. Foster City, Calif.: IDG Books Worldwide, 2000.

Internal Revenue Service, www.irs.gov, 2002.

Jessup, Claudia, and Genie Chipps. *A Woman's Guide to Starting a Business.* New York: Henry Holt and Company, 1991.

Jette, Christine. *Tarot Shadow Work.* St. Paul, Minn.: Llewellyn Publications, 2000.

———. *Tarot for All Seasons.* St. Paul, Minn.: Llewellyn Publications, 2001.

———. *Tarot for the Healing Heart.* St. Paul, Minn.: Llewellyn Publications, 2001.

Johnson, Cait. *Tarot for Every Day.* Wappinger Falls, N.Y.: Shawangunk Press, 1994.

Johnson, Cait, and Maura D. Shaw. *Tarot Games.* San Francisco: Harper San Francisco, 1994.

Judy, Stephanie. *Making Music for the Joy of It.* Los Angeles: Jeremy P. Tarcher, Inc., 1990.

Kaplan, Harold I., M.D., and Benjamin J. Sadock, M.D. *Pocket Handbook of Clinical Psychiatry.* 6th ed. Baltimore, Md.: Williams and Wilkins, 1990.

———. *Synopsis of Psychiatry.* Baltimore, Md.: Williams and Wilkins, 1991.

Kennedy, Eugene, and Sara C. Charles, M.D. *On Becoming a Counselor: A Basic Guide for Nonprofessional Counselors and Other Helpers.* 3d ed. New York: Crossroad Publishing Company, 2001.

Kobler, Ronald D., et al, eds. *Smart Computing Learning Series: Web Tools.* Lincoln, Nebr.: Sandhills Publishing Company, 2002.

Lauver, Phillip, and David R. Harvey. *The Practical Counselor: Elements of Effective Helping.* Pacific Grove, Calif.: Brooks/Cole Publishing Co., 1997.

Levinson, Jay Conrad. *Guerrilla Marketing: Secrets for Making Big Profits from Your Small Business.* New York: Houghton-Mifflin, 1998.

Lewis, Melvin, M.D., and Fred R. Volkmar, M.D. *Clinical Aspects of Child and Adolescent Development.* Philadelphia: Lea and Febiger, 1990.

Liflander, Rob. *The Everything Online Business Book: Use the Internet to Build Your Business.* Holbrook, Mass.: Adams Media Corporation, 2000.

Liszt.com, www.liszt.com, 2002.

Lloyd, Carol. *Creating a Life Worth Living.* New York: HarperCollins, 1997.

Mangold, Lori, and Scott Mangold. *The Professional Pet Sitter: A Guide to Starting and Operating a Successful Service*. Portland, Ore.: Paws-itive Press, 1995.

Marks, Tracy. *The Art of Chart Interpretation*. Sebastopol, Calif.: CRS Publications, 1986.

Milano, Carol. *HERS: The Wise Woman's Guide to Starting a Business on $2000 or Less*. New York: Allworth Press, 1991.

Moran, Patti J. *Pet Sitting for Profit*. New York: Howell Book House, 1997.

Muschla, Gary R. *Writing Workshop Survival Kit*. New York: Center for Applied Research in Education, 1993.

Nemeth, Maria, Ph.D. *The Energy of Money: A Spiritual Guide to Financial and Personal Fulfillment*. New York: Ballantine Publishing Group, 1997.

Pfaffenberger, Bryan. *Webster's New World Computer Dictionary*. New York: Hungry Minds, Inc., 2001.

Reber, Arthur S. *The Penguin Dictionary of Psychology*. New York: Penguin Books, 1985.

Sohnen-Moe, Cherie. *Business Mastery: A Guide for Creating a Fulfilling, Thriving Business and Keeping It Successful*. 3d ed. Tucson, Ariz.: Sohnen-Moe Associates, Inc., 1997.

Stanhope, Marcia, and Jeanette Lancaster. *Community Health Nursing*. 2d ed. Boston: Mosby-Year Book, Inc., 1996.

Steele, Joelle. *How to Market Your Astrological Services*. Pacific Grove, Calif.: Park Place Publications, 1998.

Storr, Anthony. *The Art of Psychotherapy*. New York: Routledge, Chapman and Hall, Inc., 1989.

Stress Management: Tips for Daily Living. A scriptographic product by Channing L. Bete Company, South Deerfield, Mass., 1999.

Syracuse, Cheryle Jones, and William Owen. *Small Business Series: Licenses, Permits And Zoning*. Columbus: Ohio State University Fact Sheet, Community Development. 2002. http://ohioline.osu.edu/cd-fact/1201.html.

Tyl, Noel. *Synthesis and Counseling in Astrology: The Professional Manual*. St. Paul, Minn.: Llewellyn Publications, 2000.

Vesey, Jason. *Uses of Computers and the Internet in the Business World.* Alma, Mich.: Alma College, 2000. http://students.alma.edu/students/02jdvese/tsld004.htm.

Wanless, James. *Strategic Intuition for the 21st Century.* Carmel, Calif: Merrill-West Publishing Company, 1996.

Index

ORDER LLEWELLYN BOOKS TODAY!

Llewellyn publishes hundreds of books on your favorite subjects! To get these exciting books, including the ones on the following pages, check your local bookstore or order them directly from Llewellyn.

Order Online:
Visit our website at www.llewellyn.com, select your books, and order them on our secure server.

Order by Phone:
- Call toll-free within the U.S. at 1-877-NEW-WRLD (1-877-639-9753) Call toll-free within Canada at 1-866-NEW-WRLD (1-866-639-9753)
- We accept VISA, MasterCard, and American Express

Order by Mail:
Send the full price of your order (MN residents add 7% sales tax) in U.S. funds, plus postage & handling to:

Llewellyn Worldwide
P.O. Box 64383, Dept. 0-7387-0217-X
St. Paul, MN 55164-0383, U.S.A.

Postage & Handling:
Standard (U.S., Mexico, & Canada). If your order is:
Up to $25.00, add $3.50
$25.01–$48.99, add $4.00
$49.00 and over, FREE STANDARD SHIPPING
(Continental U.S. orders ship UPS. AK, HI, PR, & P.O. Boxes ship USPS 1st class. Mex. & Can. ship PMB.)

International Orders:
Surface Mail: For orders of $20.00 or less, add $5 plus $1 per item ordered. For orders of $20.01 and over, add $6 plus $1 per item ordered.

Air Mail:
Books: Postage & Handling is equal to the total retail price of all books in the order.
Non-book items: Add $5 for each item.

Orders are processed within 2 business days. Please allow for normal shipping time.
Postage and handling rates subject to change.

The Complete Book of Tarot Reversals

MARY K. GREER

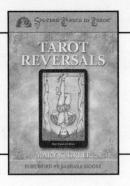

What do you do with the "other half" of a Tarot reading: the reversed cards? Just ignore them as many people do? *The Complete Book of Tarot Reversals* reveals everything you need to know for reading the most maligned and misunderstood part of a spread. These interpretations offer inner support, positive advice, and descriptions of the learning opportunities available, yet with a twist that is uniquely their own.

Enhance and deepen the quality of your consultations as you experiment with the eleven different methods of reading reversed cards. Use the author's interpretations to stimulate your own intuitive ideas. Struggle in the dark no longer.

- The author has a strong reputation with Tarot enthusiasts
- The first book to fully and exclusively address the interpretation of cards that appear upside-down in a Tarot spread
- Features eleven different methods of determining reversed card meanings
- For readers at all levels of expertise

1-56718-285-2
6 x 9, 312 pp. $14.95

To order, call 1-877-NEW-WRLD
Prices subject to change without notice

Tarot for the Healing Heart

Christine Jette

Tarot for the Healing Heart introduces a new way to use the tarot. Discover how to promote healing in yourself through the use of mind-body techniques and visualization with the cards.

Wellness is body, mind, and spirit in balance. Illness is a neutral, direct message focusing our awareness on issues that need attention. We are either in a life lesson (imbalanced energy/dis-ease) or life wisdom (balanced energy/healing) mode. The tarot can reveal areas that are out of balance and uncover ways to support the healing process. Through the suits of the tarot, you will explore illness and healing as they relate to the four levels of existence—physical (pentacles), emotional (cups), psychological (swords), and the spiritual (wands). The major arcana cards represent the higher insight of disease, and the court cards are the healers of the tarot.

Activities include ten original tarot layouts, tarot meditations for releasing the healer within, exploring healing as a lifestyle, breaking the pain cycle, contacting your healing guide, and developing psychic ability through sacred play with tarot cards. No prior knowledge of tarot is needed.

0-7387-0043-6
7½ x 9⅛, 264 pp. $14.95

To order, call 1-877-NEW-WRLD
Prices subject to change without notice

Tarot for All Seasons
Celebrating the Days & Nights of Power

CHRISTINE JETTE

Working with the tarot cards is a simple but powerful way to create a seasonal connection with the Goddess. The universal pictures of tarot awaken the voice of inner knowing as you align yourself with the larger forces of the universe and embrace the cycle of the seasons.

Part spellbook, part ritual guide, *Tarot for All Seasons* describes how to extract seasonal energy throughout the Wheel of the Year to improve all areas of your life—relationships, making money, establishing a career, and choosing healthful lifestyles. Useful for both solitary practice and coven group wisdom.

- This is the first book devoted solely to how tarot relates to the Wheel of the Year
- Addresses the common concerns and developmental stages of young women
- Combines ritual, Wiccan history, mystery and lore, focused intention (magic), and seasonal tarot layouts
- The twelve original layouts capture the spirit of the full moon esbats, waxing and waning moons, and eight solar holidays
- Readers are empowered to "change the cards to change reality"

0-7387-0105-X
6 x 9, 144 pp., illus. $12.95

To order, call 1-877-NEW-WRLD
Prices subject to change without notice

Tarot Shadow Work

Using the Dark Symbols to Heal

CHRISTINE JETTE

Within each of us, the unconscious holds our forbidden feelings, secret wishes, and creative urges. Over time, these "dark forces" take on a life of their own and form the shadow—a powerful force of unresolved inner conflicts and unexpressed emotions that defies our efforts to control it. The shadow becomes our inner saboteur, martyr, victim, addict, sadist, masochist, or tyrant.

Tarot Shadow Work shows you how to free yourself from the shadow's power. Through tarot work, journaling, meditation, creative visualization, and dream work, you will bring the shadow into the light, thus regaining your rightful place as the author of your own life.

This is not a book of traditional tarot definitions and their reversed meaning. Instead, it takes each of the twenty-two cards of the major arcana (the Fool through the World), and depicts its dual nature of life. *Tarot Shadow Work* is the only book that uses the tarot exclusively for conflict resolution and healing past hurts.

1-56718-408-1
6 x 9, 264 pp., illus. $12.95